THE UNITED NATIONS IN A TURBULENT WORLD

INTERNATIONAL PEACE ACADEMY

OCCASIONAL PAPER SERIES

THE UNITED NATIONS
IN A TURBULENT WORLD

JAMES N. ROSENAU

LYNNE RIENNER PUBLISHERS ▪ BOULDER & LONDON

Published in the United States of America in 1992 by
Lynne Rienner Publishers, Inc.
1800 30th Street, Boulder, Colorado 80301

and in the United Kingdom by
Lynne Rienner Publishers, Inc.
3 Henrietta Street, Covent Garden, London WC2E 8LU

Published for the International Peace Academy
777 United Nations Plaza
New York, New York 10017

The *International Peace Academy Occasional Paper Series* is made possible by
the support of the Ford Foundation and the Samuel Freeman Charitable Trust.

Library of Congress Cataloging-in-Publication Data
Rosenau, James N.
    The United Nations in a turbulent world / by James N. Rosenau.
        p. cm.—(International Peace Academy occasional paper series)
    Includes bibliographical references and index.
    ISBN 1-55587-330-8
    1. United Nations. 2. International relations. I. Title.
    II. Series.
    JX1977.R576 1992
    341.23—dc20   91-45522
                                                                        CIP

British Cataloguing in Publication Data
A Cataloguing in Publication record for this book
is available from the British Library.

Printed and bound in the United States of America

The paper used in this publication meets the requirements of the American
National Standard for Permanence of Paper for Printed Library Materials Z39.48-1984.

CONTENTS

1

POSING THE PROBLEM:
ENGULFED OR ENLARGED?

The American Army is better than the United Nations because they have power and have a big say. The U.N. does what? It just has a name.   —Nazar Ali, 21-year-old Kurdish refugee[1]

In a resolution approved 10 to 3, the Council dismissed Iraq's objection that its handling of the Kurdish and Shiite Muslim Arab insurgencies was an internal affair, saying the wave of refugees flowing toward neighboring Turkey and Iran threatens "international peace and security." Never before has the United Nations Security Council held that governments threaten international security if their actions force thousands of their citizens to flee to other lands.   —News report[2]

In a turbulent world of restless publics, faltering economies, widening cleavages, and vast international transformations, where does the United Nations (UN) fit? The two observations above suggest contradictory answers, with the young Kurdish refugee according little significance to the UN, while the news report implies that the UN's role is capable of considerable expansion. As expressions of skepticism and optimism about the UN's future, the two quotations summarize the tensions that presently beset international organizations (IOs) and that are the central focus of this occasional paper. They also serve to highlight the emphasis given to the relevance of citizens, both individually and collectively, to the global context in which the UN conducts its affairs.

Underlying the analysis are three overriding questions: What have been the consequences for the UN of the profound transformations the world has undergone since its creation in 1945? Can it meet the challenges posed by an increasingly turbulent world? And can the UN respond to the challenges in creative ways that enable it to serve as an agent as well as a product of global change?

The answers to these questions are not simple—as the ensuing pages demonstrate—but they are clear-cut. Among other things, the analysis leads to the unqualified conclusion that the UN is likely to benefit from the growing complexity of world affairs, from the widespread challenges to established national and subnational authorities, and from the global shift away from traditional criteria of legitimacy and toward assessments based on the adequacy of leadership performances.

The thrust of the argument also develops a clear answer to the question posed in the title of this chapter: rather than engulfing the UN, the transformations at work in world politics are viewed as enlarging its roles in a number of ways. Six recommendations are offered for seizing the opportunities to expand the UN's salience and effectiveness in the emergent global order.

Inquiries into IOs have not focused extensively on the responsiveness of the UN to the worldwide dynamics of change. Rather they have tended to proceed from the assumption that, whatever the effectiveness of IOs, they operate in an unchanging world bound by the immutable dictates of the sovereignty principle and that, therefore, the key to making IOs more effective lies in their decisionmaking procedures and institutional arrangements. Variability is thus attached to IOs and not the worlds to which they respond and seek to manage.[3] Obviously, however, the presumption of an underlying constancy in international affairs is no longer beyond question (if it ever was). There are too many signs of extensive global change to allow for the luxury of approaching the UN as if its institutions and activities are independent of the ebb and flow of world politics.

Several answers are possible to the question of how a transformed world may be transforming the UN. One posits the changes as essentially peripheral to the ongoing interstate system and thus dismisses the UN as ephemeral, as destined to function as it always has. A second accepts the premise that the huge changes have altered the nature and structure of the interstate system, but at the same time sees the UN as unable to acquire sufficient control over the course of events to act as a major change agent. In this conception the UN is viewed as still constrained by the actions of states and other global dynamics, with the result that it will either adapt its goals, tasks, structures, and procedures to the

THE UN IN A TURBULENT WORLD

transformations in world politics or become increasingly irrelevant. A third answer conceives of the global transformations as offering the UN a number of opportunities to function as an agent as well as a product of the change, thereby putting it in a position of having some influence over the course of events and the management of world affairs.

My concern here is primarily with the second and third perspectives. I will outline a number of basic structural developments that militate against the expectation that the UN will continue functioning as it always has. Then, after indicating how the transformations presently at work in the world may be impacting on the UN, I will probe the major ways in which the UN has responded to the adaptive challenges. Finally, I will move beyond the processes of adaptation and explore the ways in which the UN might also serve as a significant agent of change and thereby contribute to the emergent structures of global politics. In other words, the central concern here is to assess the extent to which the UN can successfully and creatively adapt to a rapidly changing world.

Tracing the capacity of the UN to function as an agent of change is not a simple matter. It is all too easy to construct a historical retrospective that attributes much of the evolution of world politics since 1945 to the presence and activities of the UN. One inquiry, for example, concluded that the UN has had a "far-reaching" impact, that it was a prime reason why the years since World War II have witnessed the absence of general war, the democratization of international relations, the achievement of independence by former colonies, the trend toward economic development, and the strengthening of international law.[4] On the other hand, a year later observers were noting that the UN had "fallen upon hard times in the 1980s"[5] and that there was a "widespread impression that collective conflict management by international organizations has failed."[6] Only a little while later, however, it was possible to give voice to the view that "the UN is playing an increasingly essential role in peacekeeping and peacemaking in the Third World."[7]

Such wide and quick fluctuations in assessments of the UN as a major change agent suggest the difficulty of evolving a long-run perspective on global transformations and the roles the UN can play in them. We are inclined either to locate our empirical assessments in our value preferences or to attach significance to the latest trend and allow our judgments to fluctuate with shifts in the course of events.

To avoid these pitfalls and maintain a consistent long-term perspective that is also sensitive to changing realities, three conceptual steps need to be taken: (1) be clear about the sources, nature, pace, direction, and consequences of change in world politics, (2) have an explicit understanding of how and where these dynamics can impact upon IOs in general and the UN in particular, and (3) be sufficiently aware of the tensions between change and continuity in world politics to discern potential roles the UN can play as an agent of change. These three tasks serve to organize the discussion that follows.

2

TURBULENCE IN
WORLD POLITICS

While there is no dearth of indicators—such as the launching of wars by states and their efforts to negotiate postwar arrangements—that highlight the many ways world politics is marked by continuity, it is hardly less difficult to demonstrate that huge changes have been at work in the global system, changes that are of sufficient magnitude to suggest the emergence of new global structures, processes, and patterns. The seemingly daily occurrence of unexpected developments and the numerous uncertainties that prevail in every region, if not every country, of the world are so pervasive as to cast doubt on the viability of the long-established ways in which international affairs have been conducted. It almost seems as if the anomalous event has replaced the recurrent pattern as the central tendency in world politics.

This is not the place to enumerate the many anomalous developments that point to profound and rapid change, but it is useful to recall the utter surprise that greeted the abrupt end of the Cold War. Pundits, professors, politicians, and others conversant with world politics were, literally, stunned, with none claiming to have anticipated it and with all admitting to ad hoc explanations. Since the sudden collapse of the Communist world was the culmination of dynamics that had been subtly at work for a long time, the intensity and breadth of the surprise it evoked can only be viewed as a measure of the extent to which our understandings of world politics have lagged behind the deep transformations that are altering the global landscape. Anomalies indicative of profound change began to flow well before the end of the Cold War,[8] but the series of events that transformed Eastern Europe late in 1989 surely focused attention to the presence of powerful change agents.

Indeed, more than a few observers and practitioners of world politics became so sensitive to the dynamics of change that they were quick to anticipate the emergence of a new global order and to regard the 1991 Gulf War as the first major expression of that order. Others have been more cautious, preferring simply to record their awe at the extent of the change and to leave open how it might unfold. As one analyst put it,

> Not only the configuration of great powers and their alliances but the very structure of political history has changed. . . . The very sovereignty and cohesion of states, the authority and efficacy of the governments are not what they were.
> Are we going to see ever larger and larger political units? . . . Or are we more likely going to see the break-up of several states into smaller ones? Are we going to see a large-scale migration of millions of peoples, something that has not happened since the last century of the Roman Empire? This is at least possible. The very texture of history is changing before our very eyes.[9]

Assuming that the quickening flow of anomalies preceded the end of the Cold War and the advent of the Gulf War, what gave rise to them? What underlying dynamics were eroding the long-standing patterns of world politics and fostering the evolution of new structures and processes? How can we begin to understand the emergence of a new global order at a level of deep change that is more fundamental than the advent of a Gorbachev in the Soviet Union, the refurbishing of US military capabilities under Ronald Reagan, or the sudden surge of East Germans into the West German Embassy in Hungary? How do we account, in short, for an acceleration of the pace of change in international affairs that has altered "the very texture of history"?

A full response to these queries is offered in my book *Turbulence in World Politics*, which is only summarized here to identify the ways in which the UN has been engulfed by turbulence and the points at which its capacities may have been enlarged, possibly enabling it to shape the structures and processes that are likely to emerge when the dynamics of global turbulence subside and new patterns become rooted into the ways of the world. Lest there be any terminological confusion, however, I must stress at the outset that the notion of turbulence is used here as more than a metaphor for great commotion and uncertainty. My purpose is not to wax eloquent about change, but rather to probe its underlying dynamics in a systematic way.

Put most succinctly, the precise meaning ascribed to the concept focuses on the fundamental patterns—what I call the prime parameters—that normally bind and sustain the continuities of international life. When these patterns are overcome by high degrees of complexity and dynamism—that is, when the number, density, interdependencies, and volatility of the actors who occupy the global stage undergo substantial expansion—world politics is viewed as having entered into a turbulent state.

Three global patterns are conceived to be primary: the distribution of power in world politics through which states, IOs, and other key actors respond to each other (a macro parameter); the authority relationships through which governments, multinational corporations, ethnic groups, and other large collectivities are linked to individual citizens (a macro-micro parameter); and the analytical and emotional skills of citizens through which they respond to the course of events (a micro parameter). All three of these parameters are judged to be greatly increasing in complexity and dynamism, thus leading to the conclusion that the world is presently experiencing its first period of turbulence since the era that culminated with the Treaty of Westphalia and the birth of the state system some 350 years ago.[10] Perhaps more to the point, the relative simultaneity that marks the impact of much greater complexity and dynamism on all three parameters has given rise to what might well be the central characteristic of world politics today, namely, the presence of persistent tensions between tendencies toward centralization and those that foster decentralization. Viewed in this way, for example, it is hardly anomalous that even as Yugoslavia and some of its component republics aspire to admission to the European Community (EC), so are several of those components seeking to break away from their political union. As will be seen, these interactive centralizing-decentralizing tensions are especially evident in the transformation of each of the three prime parameters.

Table 1 summarizes the changes in the three parameters, but the order of their listing should not be interpreted as implying causal sequences in which the actions of individuals are conceived to precede the behavior of collectivities. On the contrary, incisive insights into the turbulence of world politics are crucially dependent on appreciating the simultaneity of the interactions among the three parameters—on recognizing that even as individuals shape the actions and orientations of the collectivities to which they belong, so do the goals, policies, and laws of the latter shape the actions and orientations of individuals. Out of such interactions a network of causation is fashioned that is so intermeshed as to make it difficult to separate causes from effects. Indeed, much of the rapidity of the

Table 1 The Transformation of Three Global Parameters

	From	To
Micro parameter	Individuals less analytically skillful and emotionally competent	Individuals more analytically skillful and emotionally competent
Macro-micro parameter	Authority structures in place as people rely on traditional and/or constitutional sources of legitimacy to comply with directives emanating from appropriate macro institutions	Authority structures in crisis as people evolve performance criteria for legitimacy and compliance with the directives issued by macro officials
Macro parameter	Anarchic system of nation-states	Bifurcation of anarchic system into state- and multi-centric subsystems

transformations at work in world politics can be traced to the ways in which the changes in each parameter stimulate and reinforce the changes in the other two.

THE MICRO PARAMETER: A SKILL REVOLUTION

The transformation of the micro parameter is to be found in the shifting capabilities of citizens everywhere. Individuals have undergone what can properly be termed a skill revolution. For a variety of reasons, ranging from the advance of communications technology to the greater intricacies of life in an ever more interdependent world, people have become increasingly more competent in assessing where they fit in international affairs and how their behavior can be aggregated into significant collective outcomes. Included among these newly refined skills, moreover, is an expanded capacity to focus emotion as well as to analyze the causal sequences that sustain the course of events.

Put differently, it is a grievous error to assume that citizenries are a constant in politics, that the world has rapidly changed and complexity greatly increased without consequences for the individuals who comprise the collectivities that interact on the global stage. As long as people were uninvolved in and apathetic about world affairs, it made sense to treat them as a constant parameter and to look to variabilities at the macro level for explanations of what happens in world politics. Today, however, the skill revolution has expanded the learning capacity of individuals, enriched their cognitive maps, and elaborated the scenarios with which they anticipate the future. It is no accident that the squares of the world's cities have lately been filled with large crowds demanding change.

It is tempting to affirm the impact of the skill revolution by pointing to the many restless publics that have protested authoritarian rule and clamored for more democratic forms of governance. While the worldwide thrust toward an expansion of political liberties and a diminution in the central control of economies is certainly linked to citizens and publics having greater appreciation of their circumstances and rights, there is nothing inherent in the skill revolution that leads people in more democratic directions. The change in the micro parameter is not so much one of new orientations as it is an evolution of new capacities for cogent analysis. The world's peoples are not so much converging around the same values as they are sharing a greater ability to recognize and articulate their values. Thus, this parametric change is global in scope because it has enabled Islamic fundamentalists, Asian peasants, and Western sophisticates alike to serve better their respective orientations. And thus, too, the commotion in public squares has not been confined to cities in any particular region of the world. From Seoul to Prague, from Soweto to Beijing, from Paris to the West Bank, from Kuwait City to Moscow, from Belgrade to Rangoon—to mention only a few of the places where collective demands have recently been voiced—the transformation of the micro parameter has been unmistakably evident.

Equally important, evidence of the skill revolution can be readily discerned in trend data for education, television viewing, computer usage, travel, and a host of other situations in which people are called upon to employ their analytic and emotional skills. And hardly less relevant, in a number of local circumstances—from traffic jams to water shortages, from budget crises to racial conflicts, from flows of refugees to threats of terrorism—people are relentlessly confronted with social, economic, and political complexities that impel them to forgo their rudimentary premises and replace them with more elaborate conceptions of how to respond to the challenges of daily life.

This is not say that people everywhere are now equal in the skills they bring to bear upon world politics. Obviously, the analytically rich continue to be more skillful than the analytically poor. But while the gap between the two ends of the skill continuum may be no narrower than in the past, the advance in the competencies of those at every point on the continuum is sufficient to contribute to a major transformation in the conduct of world affairs. More important for present purposes, the skill revolution highlights the question of how the UN will be affected by the global expansion of analytic skills at the micro level. As will be seen, the enhanced skills of citizens offer IOs new opportunities for extending their influence if they are able to seize upon them.

THE MACRO-MICRO PARAMETER:
A RELOCATION OF AUTHORITY

This parameter consists of the recurrent orientations, practices, and patterns through which citizens at the micro level are linked to their collectivities at the macro level. In effect, it encompasses the authority relationships whereby large aggregations—private organizations as well as public agencies—achieve and sustain the cooperation and compliance of their memberships. Historically, these relationships have been founded on traditional criteria of legitimacy derived from constitutional and legal sources. Under those circumstances individuals were habituated to compliance with the directives issued by higher authorities. They did what they were told to do because, well, that is what one did. As a consequence, authority remained in place for decades, even centuries, as people unquestioningly yielded to the dictates of governments or the leadership of any other organizations with which they were affiliated. For a variety of reasons, including the expanded analytic skills of citizens and the factors noted below, the foundations of this parameter have also undergone erosion. Throughout the world today, in both public and private settings, the sources of authority have shifted from traditional to performance criteria of legitimacy.

In other words, where authority relationships were once in place, now they are in crisis, with the readiness of individuals to comply with governing directives being very much a function of their assessment of the performances of the authorities. The more the performance record is considered appropriate—in terms of satisfying needs, moving toward goals, and providing stability—the more likely they are to cooperate and comply. The less they approve the performance record, the more likely they are to withhold their compliance or otherwise complicate the efforts of macro authorities.

As a consequence of the pervasive authority crises, states and governments have become less effective in confronting challenges and implementing policies. They can still maintain public order through their police powers, but their ability to address substantive issues and solve substantive problems is declining as people find fault with their performances and thus question their authority, redefine the bases of their legitimacy, and withhold their cooperation. Such a transformation is being played out dramatically today in the Soviet Union, as it was only a few years earlier within all the countries of Eastern Europe. But authority crises in the former Communist world are only the more obvious instances of this newly emergent pattern. It is equally evident in every other part of the world, albeit the crises take different forms in different countries and different types of private organizations. In Canada the authority crisis is rooted in linguistic, cultural, and constitutional issues as Quebec seeks to secede or otherwise redefine its relationship to the central government. In France the devolution of authority was legally sanctioned through legislation that privatized several governmental activities and relocated authority away from Paris and toward greater jurisdiction for the provinces.[11] In China the provinces enjoy a wider jurisdiction by, in effect, ignoring or defying Beijing. In Yugoslavia the crisis has led to violence and civil war, as some of its component republics seek autonomy and independence. In the crisis-ridden countries of Latin America the challenge to traditional authority originates with insurgent movements or the drug trade. And in those parts of the world where the shift to performance criteria of legitimacy has not resulted in the relocation of authority—such as the United States, Israel, Argentina, the Philippines, and South Korea—uneasy stalemates prevail in the policymaking process as governments have proven incapable of bridging societal divisions sufficiently to undertake the decisive actions necessary to address and resolve intractable problems.

Nor are the global authority crises confined to states and

governments. They are also manifest in subnational jurisdictions, international organizations, and nongovernmental transnational entities. Indeed, in some cases the crises unfold simultaneously at different levels: just as the issue of Quebec's place in Canada became paramount, for example, so did the Mohawks in Quebec press for their own autonomy. Similarly, just as Moldavia recently rejected Moscow's authority, so did several ethnic groups within Moldavia seek to establish their own autonomy by rejecting Moldavia's authority. Similarly, to cite but a few conspicuous examples of crises in international and transnational organizations, UNESCO, the PLO, and the Catholic Church have all experienced decentralizing dynamics that are at least partly rooted in the replacement of traditional with performance criteria of legitimacy.

The relocating of authority precipitated by the structural crises of states and governments at the national level occurs in several directions, depending in good part on the scope of the enterprises people perceive as more receptive to their concerns and thus more capable of meeting their increased preoccupation with the adequacy of performances. In many instances this has involved "downward" relocation toward subnational groups—toward ethnic minorities, local governments, single-issue organizations, religious and linguistic groupings, political factions, trade unions, and the like. In some instances the relocating process has moved in the opposite direction toward more encompassing collectivities that transcend national boundaries. The beneficiaries of this "upward" relocation of authority range from supranational organizations like the European Community to intergovernmental organizations like the International Committee of the Red Cross, from nongovernmental organizations like Greenpeace to professional groups such as Médicins sans Frontières, from multinational corporations like IBM to inchoate social movements that join together environmentalists or women in different countries, from informal international regimes like those active in different industries to formal associations of political parties like those that share conservative or socialist ideologies—to mention but a few types of larger-than-national entities that have become the focus of legitimacy sentiments. Needless to say, these multiple directions in which authority is being relocated serve to reinforce the tensions between the centralizing and decentralizing dynamics that underlie the turbulence presently at work in world politics.

Associated with the crises that have overcome the macro-micro parameter is an undermining of the principle of national sovereignty. To challenge the authority of the state and to then redirect legitimacy sentiments toward supranational or subnational collectivities is to begin to deny that the state has the ultimate decisional power, including the right to resort to force. Since authority is structurally layered such that many levels of authority may have autonomy within their jurisdictions without also possessing sovereign powers, there is no one-to-one relationship between the location of authority and sovereignty. Nevertheless, trends toward the relocation of authority are bound to contribute to the erosion of sovereignty. If a state is thwarted in its efforts to mobilize effective armed forces, then its sovereignty is hardly a conspicuous feature of its existence as an independent collectivity. If it cannot prevent one of its subjurisdictions from seceding, then the reach of its sovereignty is certainly reduced.

In view of the centrality of Third World countries in the UN system, it is useful to note that the undermining of the sovereignty principle began with its redefinition in the decolonizing processes of the former European empires after World War II. In using self-determination as the sole criterion for statehood, irrespective of whether a former colony had the consensual foundations and resources to govern, a number of sovereign states were created, recognized, and admitted to the UN even though they were unable to develop their economies and manage their internal affairs without external assistance. As a result of these weaknesses, the value of sovereignty seemed less compelling once the struggle for independence was won and the tasks of governance were taken on. Rather than being an obvious source of strength, sovereignty thus often seemed to be less a source of independence than an invitation to interdependence.[12]

It follows that a central question in assessing whether the UN has been engulfed or enlarged by global turbulence is whether the UN is a beneficiary of the complexity and dynamism that has overtaken the macro-micro parameter and led to the relocation of authority. Or, if it is not a direct beneficiary in the sense of actually extending its authority, does it benefit indirectly from the weakening of states and the accretions of authority experienced by other types of collectivities? To what extent, in other words, has the sovereignty principle been undermined insofar as the functioning of the UN is concerned? Is the UN the last redoubt of the sovereignty principle or have its roles and capacities been altered as a consequence of the strains to which the principle has lately been subjected? Part of the answer to these questions lies in the consequences of global turbulence for the macro structures of world politics, to which we now turn.

THE MACRO PARAMETER:
A BIFURCATION OF GLOBAL STRUCTURES

For more than three centuries the overall structure of world politics has been founded on an anarchic system of sovereign nation-states that did not have to answer to any higher authority and that managed their conflicts through accommodation or war. States were not the only actors on the world stage, but traditionally they were the dominant collectivities who set the rules by which the others had to live. The resulting state-centric world evolved its own hierarchy based on the way in which military, economic, and political power was distributed. Depending on how many states had the greatest concentration of power, the overall system was varyingly marked at different historical moments by hegemonic, bipolar, or multipolar structures.

Today, however, the state-centric world is no longer predominant. Due to the skill revolution, the worldwide spread of authority crises, and several other sources of turbulence (noted below), it has undergone bifurcation. A complex multi-centric world of diverse, relatively autonomous actors has emerged, replete with structures, processes, and decision rules of its own. The sovereignty-free actors of the multi-centric world consist of multinational corporations, ethnic minorities, subnational governments and bureaucracies, professional societies, political parties, transnational organizations, and the like. Individually, and sometimes jointly, they compete, conflict, cooperate, or otherwise interact with the sovereignty-bound actors of the state-centric world.[13] Table 2 delineates the main differences between the multi-centric and state-centric worlds.

In sum, and to reiterate, while the bifurcation of world politics has not pushed states to the edge of the global stage, they are no longer the only key actors. Now they are faced with the new task of coping with disparate rivals from another world as well as the challenges posed by counterparts in their own world. The macro parameter is thus perhaps most incisively described as sustaining two worlds of world politics. Whether this bifurcated global structure facilitates or complicates the tasks of the United Nations is an issue to which much of the ensuing analysis is addressed.

Table 2 Structure and Process in the Two Worlds of World Politics

	State-centric World	Multi-centric World
Number of essential actors	Fewer than 200	Hundreds of thousands
Prime dilemma of actors	Security	Autonomy
Principal goals of actors	Preservation of territorial integrity, and physical security	Increase in world market shares, maintenance of integration of subsystems
Ultimate resort for realizing goals	Armed force	Withholding of cooperation or compliance
Normative priorities	Processes, especially those that preserve sovereignty and the rule of law	Outcomes, especially those that expand human rights, justice, and wealth
Modes of collaboration	Formal alliances whenever possible	Temporary coalitions
Scope of agenda	Limited	Unlimited
Rules governing interactions among actors	Diplomatic practices	Ad hoc, situational
Distribution of power among actors	Hierarchical by amount of power	Relative equality as far as initiating action is concerned
Interaction patterns among actors	Symmetrical	Asymmetrical
Locus of leadership	Great powers	Innovative actors with extensive resources
Institutionalization	Well established	Emergent
Susceptibility to change	Relatively low	Relatively high
Control over outcomes	Concentrated	Diffused
Bases of decisional structures	Formal authority, law	Various types of authority, effective leadership

Source: Reproduced from James N. Rosenau, *Turbulence in World Politics: A Theory of Change and Continuity* (Princeton: Princeton University Press, 1990), p. 250.

3

THE SOURCES OF
GLOBAL TURBULENCE

Given a world with the new parametric values represented by the skill revolution, the relocation of authority, and the bifurcation of global structures, it is hardly surprising that politicians, publics, and pundits speak of a new global order. For it is a new order—not so much because the Cold War ended or because a successful coalition was mobilized to oust Iraq from Kuwait, but because the fundamental underpinnings of world politics, the parameters that sustain it, have undergone transformation.

Thus far, however, the discussion has been more descriptive than explanatory. We have defined turbulence and indicated the sites at which its consequences are likely to be most extensive and enduring, but we have not accounted for the dynamics that underlie the parametric transformations. What drives the turbulence? This question needs to be clarified, at least briefly, if we are to assess the implications of the new order for the United Nations.

Although a variety of factors have contributed to the onset of turbulence, several stand out as particularly salient and worthy of elaboration. As can be seen in the enumeration that follows, some of these sources are external to the processes of world politics and some are internal to them. Together they go a long way toward explaining why what once seemed so anomalous now appears so patterned.

PROLIFERATION OF ACTORS

Perhaps few facts about world politics are better known than those that describe the huge increase in the human population since the end of World War II. Where the world's population was in excess of 2.5 billion in 1950, by 1990 the figure had passed five billion and it continues to grow at a rapid rate. This demographic explosion lies at the heart of many of the world's problems and is also a continual source of the complexity and dynamism that have overwhelmed the parameters of the global system. Ever greater numbers of people have exerted pressure for technological innovations. They have meant larger, more articulate, and increasingly unwieldly publics. They have contributed to the unmanageability of public affairs that has weakened states, stimulated the search for more responsive collectivities, and hastened the advent of paralyzing authority crises. And they have created through the sheer weight of numbers new and intractable public issues, of which famines and threats to the environment are only the more conspicuous examples.

But the proliferation of relevant actors is not confined to the huge growth in the number of individual citizens. No less important for present purposes is the vast increase in the number and types of collective actors whose leaders can clamber onto the global stage and act on behalf of their memberships. Indeed, to note that the mounting complexity of world affairs springs in part from the deepening density of the global system is to stress not so much the unorganized complexity fostered by the population explosion as it is to refer to an organized complexity consisting of millions of factions, associations, parties, organizations, movements, interest groups, and a host of other kinds of collectivities that share an aspiration to advance their welfare and a sensitivity to the ways in which a rapidly changing world may require them to network with each other.

The dizzying increase in the density of actors that sustain world politics stems, of course, from a variety of sources. In part it is a product of the trend toward ever greater specialization, the hallmark of industrial and postindustrial economies, and the greater interdependence those economies foster. In part, too, it is a consequence of widespread dissatisfaction with large-scale collectivities and the performance of existing authorities, a discontent that underlies the turn to less encompassing organizations that are more fully expressive of close-at-hand needs and wants. Relevant here also are the expanded analytic skills of citizens that enable them to appreciate how they can join in collective actions that serve as avenues for expressing their discontent. Whatever the reasons for the proliferation of collective actors, however, their sheer number has been a prime stimulus to the evolution of the multi-centric world and to the authority crises that have wracked the state-centric world.

As will be seen, the impact on the UN of this vast increase in sovereignty-free actors has been considerable. But it is no more conspicuous than the diverse ways in which the the UN has had to cope with an extensive proliferation of its own ranks.[14] On a lesser scale, the state-centric world has also undergone substantial enlargement, with the number of member states in the UN having more than tripled since its inception in 1945. Indeed, this growth has contributed to the exponential increase of actors in the multi-centric world, since each new state carved out of the former colonial empires spawned its own array of nongovernmental actors who contributed to the formation of new transnational networks. The organized complexity and deepening density of the global system, in other words, has derived from formal state-making dynamics as well as the multiplication of activities within societies.

IMPACT OF DYNAMIC TECHNOLOGIES

With the cannonball having yielded to the ballistic missile and the telegraph having given way to the fax machine, the technological explosion since World War II is no less impressive than its demographic counterpart. Where the latter has led to the crowding of geographic space, the former has fostered the narrowing of social and political space. In a wide number of fields—from agriculture to transportation, from communications to medicine, from biogenetics to artificial intelligence—technological dynamics have facilitated huge leaps in humankind's ability to overcome constraints imposed by the laws of nature: physical distances have been shortened, social distances have been contracted, and economic barriers have been circumvented. And as peoples have thus become more and more interdependent, so have enormous consequences followed for the skills of individuals, the conduct of their relations with higher authorities, and the viability of their macrocollectivities. It is highly doubtful, in short, whether world politics would have been overtaken by turbulence without the explosion of innumerable technologies since 1950.

Two of these explosions, the nuclear and communications revolutions, stand out as especially relevant to the complexity and dynamism that have inundated the three prime parameters. The extraordinary advances in military weaponry subsequent to World

War II, marked by nuclear warheads and the rocketry to deliver them, imposed a context on the conduct of world affairs that reduced the probability of a major international war. The nuclear revolution thus had the ironic consequence of inhibiting states in the use of one of their prime instruments for pursuing and defending their interests. To be sure, the arms race and events like the Cuban missile crisis infused global life with a high degree of volatility that often made it seem very fragile indeed. Nevertheless, even as the nuclear context emphasized the extraordinary capacities several states had acquired, so did it point up the limits of state action and thereby opened the door for challenges to the authority of states. It is no accident that as states added substantially to their nuclear arsenals, so did a series of transnational, large-scale, and powerful social movements—in the realms of peace, ecology, and womens' rights—acquire enough momentum to seriously challenge governments.

The communications revolution is hardly less central as a source of global turbulence. The rapidity and clarity with which ideas and information now circulate through television, VCRs, computer networks, fax machines, satellite hookups, fiber-optic telephone circuits, and many other microelectronic devices has rendered national boundaries ever more porous and world politics ever more vulnerable to cascading demands. Events that once took weeks and months to unfold now develop within days and hours. Financial transactions that once were mired in long delays can now be consummated in seconds. Diplomats, adversaries, military commanders, and publics who once had to wait long periods before reaching conclusions are now able to act decisively. Today the whole world, its leaders and its citizenries, instantaneously share the same pictures and descriptions, albeit not necessarily the same understandings, of what is transpiring in any situation.[15]

Examples of the cascading effects of the communications revolution abound. Most conspicuous perhaps is the impact of the Cable News Network (CNN), which is said to be on and continuously watched in every embassy and every foreign office of every country in the world and which during the Gulf War served as the basis for diplomatic and military action on both sides of the conflict.[16] Hardly less telling is the example of the French journal *Actuel*, which was so upset by the crackdown in Tiananmen Square that, having compiled a mock edition of the *People's Daily* that contained numerous accounts the Chinese leadership did not want their people to read, sent it to every fax machine in China in the fall of 1989.[17] Or consider the explosive implications of the fact that 5 percent of Brazil's households had television receiving sets when its 1960 presidential election was held and that this figure had swollen to 72 percent at the time of the next presidential contest in 1989.

Given the magnitude of these communications dynamics, it is hardly surprising that people everywhere have become more analytically skillful, more ready to challenge authority, and more capable of engaging in collective actions that press their demands. Their information may be skewed and their understanding of the stakes at risk in situations may be loaded with bias, but the stimuli to action are now ever present. Today individuals can literally see the aggregation of demands and how the participation of their counterparts elsewhere can have meaningful consequences. Likewise, the availability of high-tech communications equipment has enabled leaders in the public and private sectors to turn quickly to their memberships and mobilize them in support of their immediate goals in the multi- and state-centric worlds.[18]

GLOBALIZATION OF NATIONAL ECONOMIES

If the communications revolution has been a prime stimulus of the tendencies toward decentralization through the empowering of citizens and subnational groups, the dynamics at work in the economics realm are equally powerful as sources of the centralizing tendencies. Starting in the technologically most advanced sectors of the global economy, and following the economic crisis of 1973-1974, a new kind of production organization geared to limited orders for a variety of specialized markets began to replace the large plants that produced standardized goods. Consequently, with the products of numerous semiskilled workers brought together in big plants no longer competitive with the outputs of a large number of small units that could be tailored to shifting demands, business became concerned about restructuring capital so as to be more effective in world markets. And as capital became increasingly internationalized, so did groups of producers and plants in different territorial jurisdictions become linked in order to supply markets in many countries, all of which fostered and sustained a financial system global in scope and centered in major cities such as New York, Tokyo, and Frankfurt.

In short, capital, production, labor, and markets have all been globalized to the point where financiers, entrepreneurs, workers, and consumers are now deeply enmeshed in networks of the world economy that have superseded the traditional political jurisdictions of national scope. Such a transformation was bound to impact upon the established parameters of world politics. Among other things, it served to loosen the ties of producers and workers to their states, to expand the horizons within which citizens pondered their self-interests, and to foster the formation of transnational organizations that could operate on a global scale to protect and advance the economic interests of their members. The rapid growth and maturation of the multi-centric world can in good part be traced to the extraordinary dynamism and expansion of the global economy. And so can the weakening of the state, which is no longer the manager of the national economy and has become, instead, an instrument for adjusting the national economy to the exigencies of an expanding world economy.

The question arises as to whether the globalization of national economies may not open up new roles for the UN to play in affecting the course of world economics. As will be seen, this is one centralizing tendency that seems unlikely to extend to the UN, if only because it involves private activities in those sectors of the multi-centric world where the UN cannot claim any legitimacy. Agencies of the UN frame codes for the conduct of transnational business, gather data on the functioning of various economic sectors, study problems of development, and otherwise facilitate international commerce,[19] but on such large questions as fluctuating interest rates, currency crises, and market shares, its specialized agencies and other IOs play only peripheral roles at most, and there is little reason to expect any changes in this regard. On the other hand, if the consequences of the globalization of national economies are assessed in terms of the number, composition, activities, and loyalties of collective actors, the conditions under which the UN performs its tasks will surely be affected.

ADVENT OF INTERDEPENDENCE ISSUES

But the evolution of the world economy is not the only source of centralizing tendencies at work in global life. There are also a number of new, transnational problems that are crowding high on the world's agenda and forcing the globalization of certain kinds of issues. Where political agendas used to consist of issues that governments could cope with on their own or through interstate bargaining, now these conventional issues are being joined by challenges that by their very nature do not fall exclusively within the jurisdiction of states and their diplomatic institutions. Six current challenges are illustrative: environmental pollution, currency crises, the drug trade, terrorism, AIDS, and the flow of refugees. Each of these issues embraces processes that involve participation by large numbers of citizens and that inherently and inescapably transgress national boundaries—the winds at Chernobyl, for example, carried the pollution into many countries and intruded upon many lives, ranging from the immediate impact on Lapps in northern Norway who were unable to market reindeer meat, to the long-term impact on thousands whose lives may be shortened by that single nuclear disaster—and thus make it impossible for governments to treat them as domestic problems or to address them through conventional diplomatic channels.

Since they are essentially the product of dynamic technologies and the shrinking social and geographic distances that separate peoples, such problems can appropriately be called "inter-dependence" issues. And, given their origins and scope, they can also be regarded as important centralizing dynamics in the sense that they impel cooperation on a transnational scale. All six issues, for instance, are the focus of either transnational social movements or ad hoc international institutions forged to ameliorate, if not to resolve, the boundary-crossing problems they have created.

The advent of interdependence issues has contributed to the present era of turbulence in world politics in several ways. First, as in the case of the economic changes, such issues have given citizens pause about their states as the ultimate problem solver and, in the case of those who join social movements, they have reoriented people to ponder a restructuring of their loyalties. In so doing, interdependence issues have also fostered the notion that transnational cooperation can be as central to world politics as interstate conflict. Equally important, given their diffuse, boundary-crossing structure, these types of issues are spawning a whole range of transnational associations that are furthering the density of the multi-centric world and, as a result, are likely to serve as additional challenges to the authority of states. In short, the structure and content of interdependence issues lend themselves well to the involvement of IOs.

WEAKENING OF STATES AND
THE RESTRUCTURING OF LOYALTIES

Inasmuch as the United Nations was created by states and continues to be viewed as an instrument of states, it is important to be clear about what is meant by the weakening of states and how the loosening of their controls has contributed to the onset of global turbulence. Since several times we have noted that these primary political actors have suffered a loss in their authority, and since their relevance to world politics and the future of the UN is so great, further precision on the matter can usefully be undertaken.

But first it must be stressed that the changing role of the state is not self-evident. States have not become peripheral to global affairs. On the contrary, they continue to maintain their world and its international system, and in so doing they continue to infuse it with vitality and a capacity for adapting to change. More than that, states have been and continue to be a source of the turbulent changes that are at work. After all, it was the state-centric and not the multi-centric world that created multilateral organizations, that developed the arrangements through which the nuclear revolution has been contained, that responded to the demands for decolonization in such a way as to produce the hierarchical arrangements that have enabled the industrial countries to dominate those in the Third World, and that framed the debate over the distribution of the world's resources—to mention only a few of the more obvious ways in which states have shaped and still shape the ongoing realities of world politics. To discern a decline in the capacity of states, therefore, is not to suggest or in any way imply that they are no longer relevant actors on the world stage. As will be seen, several of the policy recommendations set forth below may well founder because states retain the capacity to resist as well as stimulate changes that affect the structures of world politics.

Indeed, some analysts see states as increasingly robust and explicitly reject the patterns highlighted here.[20] This reasoning posits the state as so deeply ensconced in the routines and institutions of politics, both domestic and international, that the erosion of its capabilities and influence is unimaginable. The state has proven itself, the argument goes, by performing vital functions that serve the needs of people, which is why it has been around more than three hundred years. In its longevity, moreover, the state has overcome all kinds of challenges, many of which are far more severe than the globalization of national economies and the emergence of new types of collectivities. Indeed, the argument concludes, there are all kinds of ways in which states may actually be accumulating greater capabilities.

This is, of course, not the occasion to amplify a refutation of such a perspective. Suffice it to say that it seems just as erroneous to treat states as constants as it is to view the skills of citizens as invulnerable to change. States are not eternal verities; they are as susceptible to variability as any other social system, and this includes the possibility of a decline in the sovereignty principle from which they derive their legitimacy as well as an erosion of their ability to address problems, much less to come up with satisfactory solutions to them.[21]

Viewed from the perspective of vulnerabilities, the growing density of populations, the expanding complexity of the organized segments of society, the globalization of national economies, the constraint of external debts, the relentless pressure of technological innovations, the challenge of subgroups intent upon achieving greater autonomy, and the endless array of other intractable problems that comprise the modern political agenda, it seems evident that world politics has cumulated to a severity of circumstances that lessens the capacity of states to be decisive and efficient. Their agendas are expanding, but they lack the will, competence, and resources to expand correspondingly. Consequently, most states are overwhelmed, unable to relieve their systemic overload to the point where effective management is possible. And added to these difficulties is the fact that citizenries, through the microelectronic revolution, are continuously exposed to the scenes of authority crises elsewhere in the world, scenes that are bound to give rise to doubts and demands in even the most stable of polities and thus to foment a greater readiness to question the legitimacy of governmental policies. There is considerable evidence, for example, that the collapse of authority in East Germany in the fall of 1989 was stimulated by the televised scenes of authority being challenged in Tiananmen Square several months earlier.[22]

Accordingly, while states may not be about to exit from the political stage, and while they may even continue to occupy the center of the stage, they do seem likely to become increasingly vulnerable and impotent. And as such, as ineffective managers of their own affairs, they also serve as stimuli to turbulence in world politics—as sources of autonomy in the multi-centric world, of internal challenges to established authority, and of more analytically skillful citizens demanding more effective performances from their leaders.

But this argument for diminished state competence is subtle and depends on a lot of intangible processes for which solid indicators are not easily developed. Perhaps most notable in this regard are subtle shifts in loyalties that accompany the globalization of the national economies, the decentralizing tendencies toward subgroup autonomy, and the emergence of performance criteria of legitimacy. Such circumstances seem bound to affect loyalties to the state. That is, as transnational and subnational actors in the multi-centric world become increasingly active and effective, as they demonstrate a capacity to deal with problems that states have found intractable or beyond their competence, citizens will begin to look elsewhere than the national capital for assistance. Examples abound. Most notable in the current period are the difficult choices that citizens of the former Soviet Union had to make between their long-standing orientations toward the Kremlin and the "downward" pull of the particular republics or ethnic minorities to which they also belonged. With the Kremlin unable to halt and reverse a steep decline in the Soviet economy, and with their subnational attachments being thereby heightened, individuals all over that troubled land had to face questions about their distant attachments that they had long taken for granted. Bankers in the Russian Republic, for instance, had to confront a difficult situation in 1990, when the republic's Parliament voted to cut its share of the Soviet budget: normally the taxes for the Soviet Union were deposited in the republic banks, which then transferred them to the coffers of the central government; but in this instance the bankers were told not to transfer the full amounts while getting pressure to do so from authorities in the central government.

It would be a mistake, however, to regard the loyalty problem as confined to multiethnic systems. Relatively homogeneous societies are beset with the same dilemma. Consider the situation of Norway, whose people have a deep emotional and historical attachment to the idea of independence. In 1972 they voted, by a small margin, not to join the European Community, but by 1990 they were faced with the possibility of being the only West European country outside the EC as Sweden, Austria, Finland, and even Switzerland either applied for membership or indicated a readiness to forgo their traditional neutrality and seek admission to the EC. Norwegian loyalties, in other words, are being pulled in an "upward" direction as the economic advantages of membership in a supranational organization increasingly challenge the psychologically satisfying and historically demonstrated virtues of being a member of an autonomous national community.[23] Or ponder the unfolding malaise in France, where a mood of pessimism is widespread and where "many Frenchmen have doubts about the capacity of their country to meet successfully the dangers, opportunities, and uncertainties which the future holds." Put even more succinctly, France is presently marked by a pervasive impression that "something is breaking apart, that society is decomposing," and that, indeed, "all the institutions built over the past 40 years are in crisis and are therefore incapable of responding."[24]

This is not to say that traditional national loyalties are being totally abandoned. Plainly, such attachments do not suddenly collapse. Rather, it is only to take note of subtle processes whereby what was once well established and beyond question is now problematic and undergoing change. Even more relevantly, it seems reasonable to presume that the diminished competence of states to act decisively, combined with the processes of loyalty transformation, serve as a significant source of the dynamics that are rendering more complex each of the three prime parameters of world politics. Clearly, the viability of the multi-centric world, the persistence of authority crises, and the analytic skills of individuals are all intensified the more the capabilities of states decline and the more the loyalties of citizens become problematic. Whether these subtle processes can also serve as a feeding ground for the United Nations to acquire more authority and to become the focus of loyalty for more individuals is, obviously, another question that needs to be considered in due course.

SUBGROUPISM

Since there is a widespread inclination to refer loosely to "nationalism" as a source of the turbulent state of world politics, it is perhaps useful to be more precise about the collective nature of those decentralizing tendencies wherein individuals and groups feel readier to challenge authority and reorient their loyalties. As previously noted, the authority crises that result from such challenges can be either of an "upward" or a "downward" kind, depending on whether the aspiration is to relocate authority in more or less encompassing jurisdictions than those that operate at the national level.[25] In a number of instances of both kinds of relocation, the motivation that sustains them is not so deeply emotional as to qualify as an "ism." The creation of subnational administrative divisions, for example, can stem from detached efforts to rationalize the work of a governmental agency or private organization, and the process of implementing the decentralized arrangements can occur in the context of reasoned dialogue and calm decisionmaking. Often, however, intense concerns and powerful attachments can accompany the press for new arrangements—feelings and commitments strong enough to justify regarding the upward relocations as evoking "transnationalism," "supranationalism," or "internationalism." The downward relocations marked by comparable intensities are perhaps best labeled with the generic term "subgroupism."

Framed concisely, subgroupism refers to those deep affinities people develop toward the close-at-hand associations, organizations, and subcultures with which they have been historically, professionally, economically, socially, or politically linked and to which they attach their highest priorities. Subgroupism values the in-group over the out-group, sometimes treating the two as adversaries and sometimes positing them as susceptible to extensive cooperation. Subgroupism can derive from and be sustained by a variety of sources, not the least being disappointment in— and alienation from—the performances of the whole system in which the subgroup is located. Most of all perhaps, its intensities are the product of long-standing historical roots that span generations and that get reinforced by an accumulated lore surrounding past events in which the subgroup survived trying circumstances.

That subgroupism can be deeply implanted in the con-sciousness of peoples is manifestly apparent in the resurfacing of strong ethnic identities throughout Eastern Europe and the former Soviet Union when, after decades, the authoritarian domination of Communist parties came to an end. In those cases, the subgroups were historic nations, and the accompanying feelings can thus be readily regarded as expressions of nationalism. Not all, or even a preponderance, of these decentralizing tendencies attach to nations, however. Governmental subdivisions, political parties, labor unions, churches, professional societies, and a host of other types of subgroups can also evoke intense attachments, and it would grossly understate the relevance of the decentralizing tendencies at work in world politics to ignore these other forms of close-at-hand ties. Accordingly, it seems preferable to regard the emotional dimensions of the generic decentralizing tendencies as those of sub-groupism and to reserve the concept of nationalism for those subgroup expressions that revolve around nations and feelings of ethnicity.

THE SPREAD OF HUNGER,
POVERTY, AND THE THIRD WORLD

Underlying the bifurcation of world politics into state- and multi-centric worlds has been another split—between industrially developed and underdeveloped countries—that has also contributed substantially to the onset of turbulence. Indeed, one could readily develop a typology based on a four-way division of international affairs in which the First and Third Worlds are each conceived in terms of state- and multi-centric subdivisions. This has not been done here because the bifurcation associated with the macro parameter is global in scope, whereas the distinction between the First and Third Worlds is more in the nature of a regional split. It is nonetheless important to note that the advent of the Third World, its terrible problems and thwarted aspirations, has been a major source of the parametric transformations that are presently roiling international affairs. Among other things, the diverse and numerous countries of the Third World have added to the complexity and dynamism of global structures; sharpened performance criteria of legitimacy; enriched the analytic skills of the underprivileged; hastened the transnationalization of economies, corporations, and social movements; limited the authority of First World states over their production facilities; intensified the flow of people from South to North; lengthened the list of interdependence issues; and strengthened the tendencies toward subgroupism.

The impact of the split fostered by the breakup of Europe's colonial empires is perhaps most obvious with respect to the global distribution of power. Not only did decolonialization result in the proliferation of actors in the state-centric world, but it also infused a greater rigidity in the hierarchy of the state-centric world. The process whereby ever greater power accompanied the emergence of industrial states in the First World was not matched when statehood came to Africa and Asia. The newly established states of the Third World acquired sovereignty and international recognition even though they lacked the internal resources and consensual foundations to provide for their own development, a circumstance that led one astute observer to call them "quasi-states"[26] and led the states themselves into a deep resentment over their dependence on the industrialized world for trade, technology, and many of the other prerequisites necessary to fulfill their desire for industrial development. Thus, as previously noted, their sovereignty can be regarded as "negative" in that it protects them against outside interference but does not empower them to address their problems successfully.[27] The result has been a pervasive global pattern in which the industrial world has continued to prosper while the Third World has languished, thus endlessly reinforcing the inequities that underlie the hierarchical structures of world politics. And having long remained at or below·the poverty line, most quasi-states and most of the Third World have been keenly aware of the inequities and have sought vainly to overcome them in a variety of ways.

Put in terms of the bifurcation model, the quasi-states legally enjoy full membership in the state-centric world, but politically, socially, and economically they have had to seek assistance in the multi-centric world. To cope with these bifurcated arrangements, for example, the states of the Third World have turned both to and on various agencies of the UN system. They have turned to the General Assembly and the Economic and Social Council (ECOSOC) for support in protecting and advancing their collective needs, and they have turned on the Security Council for failing to meet these needs, for having become an instrument of their domination by the First World. For many Third-Worlders the UN is an integral part of the system of domination that marks global structures, and thus many would doubtless react to the proposals derived from the turbulence model (below) for making the UN a more effective agent of change as simply more of the same, as misplaced idealism that amounts to little more than techniques for maintaining their subordination. As they see it, bifurcation means the perpetuation of hierarchy, and hierarchy means that power is continuously and relentlessly being exercised against them.[28]

Whatever may be the validity of this perspective, it has also served as a source of the transformation in the macro-micro parameter. Third World resentments, the legitimacy problems of quasi-states, and their attempts to use their majority in the General Assembly to alter the UN's agenda and priorities have extended and deepened the global authority crisis. Indeed, the UN has become a major site of the authority crisis as the Third World has challenged the legitimacy of its actions and as the First World, fearful of dominance by the Third World, has also questioned its legitimacy by periodically failing to meet its financial obligations to the UN.

Even as the advent of the Third World has rigidified the hierarchical structure of the state-centric world, so has it added to the decentralizing tendencies in the multi-centric world. Composed of tribes and ethnic groups artificially brought together under state banners by First World decolonizers, besieged by multinational corporations seeking to extend their operations and markets, and plagued with internal divisions and massive socioeconomic problems, Third World countries have added greatly to the breadth and depth of the multi-centric world. Their quasi-sovereignty keeps them active in the state system, but the multi-centric world has been hospitable to their fragmenting dynamics and thereby contributed to the process wherein subgroup networks are proliferating.

4

THE UN AS A
PRODUCT OF CHANGE

Whatever may be the limitations of casting the turbulence model at a high level of abstraction, it has the virtue of freeing us to ask a number of specific questions that have not been previously explored. Most notably, it frees us from the assumption that the UN is so thoroughly mired in the sovereignty principle that it has been and continues to be impervious to fundamental change. That is, at a time when authority relationships throughout the world are in flux and undergoing relocation, when the capacities of states are diminishing, it seems unimaginable that the UN has not been affected. The questions follow:

• Has the UN benefited from the advent of bifurcation and the greater autonomy of actors in the multi-centric world in the sense that it, too, has greater autonomy, that its agencies and officials are now major players in the multi-centric world even as they remain products and agents of the state-centric world?

• Has the diminishing capacities of states fostered a relocation of some authority in the United Nations and a readiness on the part of its agencies to ignore, circumvent, or otherwise challenge the sovereignty principle?

• If legitimacy and authority now rest more on performance than on traditional criteria, does this not suggest considerable potential for the UN if its activities are marked by success? What does it imply if the UN's record is one of repeated failure?

• Does the proliferation of subgroups and the ethnic and communal conflicts that divide them serve to weaken international institutions and render the UN ever more ineffective? Or has the advent of more numerous groups increasingly free of state controls facilitated the work of UN agencies?

• Will the expanding skills of citizens contribute to a lifting of their own horizons that enhances the status of UN programs and peacemaking activities?

• Will the analytic habits of UN personnel prove sufficiently flexible to enable them to take advantage of the new opportunities afforded by the bifurcation of world politics, the erosion of sovereignty principle, and the other uncertainties that are the heir of global turbulence? Or will their habits be too rooted in old premises, with the result that the centralizing dynamics at work in the world will find expression in new international regimes and regional institutions that, in effect, bypass the UN?

• Could it be that the world is on the verge of a drastically new global order in which IOs are increasingly foci of important decisions as they move more effectively on the world stage, intrude more fully into the internal affairs of states, and thereby encourage the spread of global norms in socioeconomic realms as well as in the field of human rights?

• If it is concluded that UN agencies and officials are well situated to seize the initiative and give direction to the management of global turbulence, what policy recommendations seem appropriate to facilitate such an outcome?

• In short, given a rapidly changing global system whose long-established parameters have been assaulted and transformed—and replaced by a bifurcated world where authority is problematic and citizens are increasingly competent—where does the UN fit? To what extent has it adapted to the changes?

To undertake to answer these questions is not only to assume that the dynamics and changes induced by global turbulence have in fact occurred and are still unfolding; it is also to break with old analytic habits, to break out of the conceptual jail that posits the UN as exclusively located in the state-centric world and bound by the sovereignty principle and its Charter to moderate, even oppose, challenges from actors or situations in the multi-centric world. More than that, to probe these questions is to escape from the even more sturdy fortress that treats deviations from the sovereignty principle as merely occasions when it serves the interests of the superpowers to act in concert or those atypical moments in history when it is convenient for states, especially the permanent members of the Security Council, to converge around a course of action that transgresses the prohibition against interfering in the domestic affairs of states. To see the UN as always subordinate to the sovereignty principle and always acting only at the convenience of states, in other words, is to assume that every situation is independent of prior situations, that learning does not occur, that precedents never get established, and that the memory bank of states is emptied after the conclusion of each situation. Put more concretely, to break from such assumptions is to entertain the possibility that members of the state system are being swept along by the turbulence that has engulfed world politics and by the emergence of new norms that are undermining the sovereignty principle to the point where it is reasonable to shift from a convenience-of-the-states explanation of concerted UN action to a states-sometimes-feel-obliged-to-go-along perspective.

Difficult as it may be to proceed in this manner, there are good reasons to do so. These reasons can be readily discerned if one plays the mental game of imagining that the UN had resisted change since its inception, that it had compiled a record of maladaptation with respect to the emergent global order wrought by the transformations of the three global parameters. The game is easy to play: a maladaptive UN would be mired in the sovereignty principle, unable to engage in peacekeeping, peacemaking, peace enforcing, peace building, or other forms of humanitarian activities because one or another state felt threatened by its intrusion and thus objected; a maladaptive UN across the decades would not have allowed for the periodic expansion of the Secretary General's activities and influence; a maladaptive UN would not have evolved an elaborate, if not always efficient, administrative machinery for undertaking social, economic, and developmental activities in a variety of fields.

None of these imagined consequences of maladaptation, of course, have occurred. Notwithstanding enormous obstacles, the UN has recorded a history of engaging in peacekeeping; its Secretary General has become a primary actor on the world stage; its administrative machinery has proliferated. To be sure, these steps beyond the sovereignty principle have been slow and erratic, but the trendline is there. The UN has been responsive to change. Its institutions have been adaptive. Its decisionmaking procedures have demonstrated a "notable elasticity" in coping with situations that cannot be attributed to its Charter and that, indeed, have reached the point where it "is now difficult to formulate a precise definition—or the limits—of what [the UN's] functions may be."[29]

As will be seen, this is not to deny a real, powerful tension in the UN between its constitutional prohibitions against interference in the domestic affairs of its member states and the turbulent circumstances that encourage its interference. It is only to assert that the trendline depicts the tension being increasingly resolved in the favor of interference. Reinforced by this conclusion, it is reasonable to explore the questions set forth above.

THE UN AS A BENEFICIARY OF BIFURCATION

Even as the proliferation of actors on the world stage and the resulting expansion of the multi-centric world have posed new and difficult problems for the UN, so have these developments served to enhance its status. For the more dense the global stage has become, the more the UN has stood out as a refuge for the unfamiliar, as the only actor that can address interdependence issues that fall outside the exclusive jurisdiction of states. The latter can resort to diplomatic channels and undertake to reach agreements with each other on such issues, but since these are issues that affect communities everywhere, eventually they are likely to be brought to the attention of the relevant UN agencies or any other IOs that may have an interest in them.[30] In the case of some issues, moreover, the demands of citizens may be so difficult for states to meet that they siphon them off to IOs, treating the latter as, so to speak, dumping grounds for unpopular problems for which there are no easy solutions.

Thus, it is hardly surprising that the UN has increasingly moved into the multi-centric world as one of its major players, even though it also continues as a product and agent of the state-centric world. And, more importantly, the more central it becomes in the former world, the more autonomy it achieves in the latter. States do not have the capacity to be involved in the wide array of problems that comprise the global agenda, so that in acknowledging the UN's capacity in this regard they have, perhaps unintentionally, allowed the UN to augment its autonomy and centrality.

Actually, the UN has long had extensive links to the sovereignty-free actors of the multi-centric world. Article 71 of its Charter accords them ("non-governmental organizations," or NGOs) a formal consultative relationship to the UN, and in subsequent decades this relationship has evolved to the point where NGOs can justifiably be viewed as "important partners of the UN, rather than as second-class citizens or poor relations."[31] It must be noted, however, that the NGOs that are formally tied to the UN system constitute only a small fraction of the sovereignty-free actors who populate the multi-centric world. The number of organizations whose relationship to the UN is formally approved by its agencies is not small, and the global influence of many of them is not trivial,[32] but nevertheless they amount to just a tiny proportion of the vast array of subnational and transnational sovereignty-free actors who have swollen the density of the multi-centric world. Indeed, in some respects the influence of the latter may be as great as that exercised by those in the UN system. NGO affiliation with the UN system normally requires consultation with, and thus approval by, the member state where the NGO has its headquarters, a requirement that nests these NGOs deep in the sovereignty world of states and binds them closely to its agenda. Since the accreditation processes invoke the rule of sovereignty and, in effect, allow states to veto the admission of NGOs they oppose, requests for NGO status have frequently precipitated intergovernmental conflicts over the merits of the applicants. On the other hand, those collectivities that do not have to go through the approval process may be better situated to press their own agenda and exercise influence indirectly through their own governments or directly through joining with social movements to mobilize citizens on behalf of their goals.

All in all, in short, the growing density of the multi-centric world seems bound to make the UN and its agencies increasingly salient as an arena for considering issues with which national governments cannot cope. And in fact the UN has in this fashion compiled an admirable record of moving into a number of situations—from refugees to famine relief, from the eradication of disease to the setting of work standards—that involve the kind of altruistic politics to which the state-centric world is not closely attuned and that might have otherwise been neglected.

THE EROSION OF THE SOVEREIGNTY PRINCIPLE

While a steady diminution of the sovereignty principle as a consequence of the bifurcation of the global system enables the UN to move more autonomously in the multi-centric world, it does not necessarily follow that its agencies act more independently in the state-centric world. They are, after all, the creatures of the state-centric world. Their mandates and funds originate with states and their activities are monitored by states, and they are thus ever subject to the whims, preferences, and biases of states. The recent history of UNESCO offers a vivid example of what can happen to a UN agency when key actors in the state-centric world make further support conditional on compliance with their demands.

Yet, the lessened independence and greater interdependence of states has opened up the possibility that they may be somewhat weakened in their capacity to monitor and offset the directives of UN officials. Or at least the erosion of the sovereignty principle has rendered more subject to interpretation what the UN's mandates are. A vacuum, as it were, has come to surround the sovereignty principle in the sense that the boundaries that divide the affairs of states and those of the UN are no longer clear-cut. Whether UN agencies dare to move into that vacuum and risk the opprobrium of states depends in large part on the predispositions of their officials—on whether Secretaries General are ready to interpret their role in situations as allowing them to undertake actions that have the effect of modifying the sovereignty principle, or whether they will conclude it is more diplomatic not to intrude in the long-standing domains of states. While some past Secretaries General may not have even recognized the availability of the former option, the advent of the changes wrought by turbulence seems likely to make future Secretaries General more conscious that a choice exists, that they may be able to move into the vacuum.[33] As will be seen, the existence of this choice highlights the importance of the criteria and procedures employed to appoint new occupants of the Secretary General's office when it becomes vacant.

It should be added that the leaders of national governments are also aware of the vacuum surrounding their sovereignty and that therefore the chances of Secretaries General successfully moving into it are likely to be greater on those occasions when chiefs of state may be open to such a move. As one observer put it, using a different but apt metaphor, "The vessel of sovereign statehood is leaky; the pumps still work from time to time, but not consistently; the captain is not sure whether to beach the vessel or to join a fleet of similarly damaged ships sailing under negotiated orders."[34]

THE UN AS A LOCUS OF AUTHORITY

The erosion of the sovereignty principle also highlights the balance of authority between the UN and its member states. Sovereignty involves the concentration of final authority, and with states experiencing increasing difficulties in exercising that kind of authority, it becomes easier to entertain the possibility that some part of the resulting vacuum might be filled by the UN. Of course, it is one thing for the UN to have become increasingly autonomous and influential in the multi-centric world and for the range of discretion open to its officials to have extended into the domain of states, but it is quite another matter to conclude that the UN is acquiring greater authority—even if only incrementally at a slow rate—in either or both of the two worlds of world politics.

Given the history of IOs and the constitutive presumption of sovereignty accruing to their members, it may seem naive, idealistic, or otherwise far-fetched even to explore whether the actions of the UN have begun to have an authoritative ring to them. As noted, there is no escaping that the UN is an organization legitimized, funded, and otherwise sustained by states and their governments and that its actions remain subject to negation by its members. Yet, at a time when authority structures around the world are in crisis, when the criteria of legitimacy are undergoing redefinition, and when authority is undergoing relocation in diverse directions, scenarios that depict accretions of authority on the part of IOs certainly become increasingly plausible.

That the derivation of such scenarios from the course of recent events is nonetheless difficult, inhibited by a fear of being interpreted as raw idealism, needs to be emphasized. The habit of treating the UN as above all a state-dominated organization is deeply engrained, and those who perceive evidence to the contrary are ever prey to a sense that they are allowing their values to govern their judgments. Indeed, there is a tendency to compensate for such perceptions by leaning over backwards to demonstrate one's proper credentials through an introductory observation to the effect that, without question, the UN is a creature of the states that sustain it. One thoughtful observer, for example, discerns that "the range of issues articulated by the UN system is astounding" even as he initiates his analysis with the caveat that state dominance of the UN is "beyond dispute here."[35] Another long-time student of the UN expresses the contradiction between his established analytic habits and his more recent empirical insights by noting at one point that "the ultimate outcome of the struggle over allocative authority is not now predictable" and then later makes, in effect, a prediction: "Although the picture is blurred and in many places hard to decipher, there has been a movement away from the decentralized system of respect for sovereignty and toward a more centralized system of decision that in some respects approaches being international governance."[36] It is almost as if the ambivalence of observers leads them to a reluctance to discern a slow accretion of authority by the UN out of fear that to do so is somehow to jeopardize the process of accretion, as if state officials might read their interpretations and be led to tighten their surveillance of UN words and actions.

A good part of the problem is that the UN is not a unitary actor. It is more accurate, rather, to refer to it as the UN system, which, like governments, consists of executive, legislative, administrative, and judicial agencies at its center and numerous specialized agencies in the field that are relatively autonomous of its central organs. All told, a full diagram of the vast array of specialized agencies, programmes, regional commissions, functional commissions, special funds, ad hoc bodies, and offices that comprise the UN system would include more than fifty distinct units, some thirty of which have executive heads that are subject to periodic election or appointment.[37] The degree of authority that attaches to the various units, of course, differs considerably, varying inversely with the degree to which they are dominated by national governments. The administrative responsibilities of the UN's Secretary General and the veto powers of the permanent members of the Security Council are illustrative of the two extremes of this continuum. Ranging between the two poles are the issues that various UN agencies have been mandated to address and ameliorate.

Some analysts contend that an inverse relationship also prevails between the salience of an issue and the authority particular UN organs can exercise with respect to it, with national governments being reluctant to authorize UN actions in situations they regard as of critical importance.[38] Others are not so sure, arguing that the UN is granted authority to address some high-salience issues when governments have a need to resolve them but either lack the capacity to do so on their own or fear getting enmeshed in an intractable situation.[39] The Suez crisis of 1956, the continuing Greek-Turkish conflict over Cyprus, Iraq's invasion of Kuwait in 1990, and the 1991 civil war in Yugoslavia are quintessential examples of these practices.

Clearly, then, whatever may be the soundness of the law of inverse salience, the question of whether authority has shifted in the direction of the UN during this turbulent period cannot be treated as a simple matter. The flow of authority can be depicted by many trendlines, depending on which UN agencies and which issue areas are being assessed. Viewed in this way, it seems clear that the aforenoted ambivalence about discerning an accretion of authority by the UN focuses mainly on those issues where the decisionmaking process is least centralized and states adhere closely to a self-interested view of their role, vetoing or voting against UN authority when it impinges on their sovereign prerogatives. Put more precisely, the fear of straying from a state-dominant conception of the UN has been most notable with respect to issues pertaining to the use of force, property rights, codes for transnational corporations, and sovereignty over resources, whereas the UN's history is marked by a more discernible trend toward greater authority with respect to social issues such as food aid, refugees, and human rights.

In pondering such issue-area differences, it is useful to note that authority need not be linked to the capacity to enforce decisions. This link tends to come to mind in connection with the notion of sovereign authority, which entitles the sovereign to resort to force to bring about desired results. But such a conception is misleadingly narrow. More often than not, political authorities are able to exercise authority without explicating that their directives may ultimately be backed with force. The key to discerning the presence or absence of effective authority, in other words, is to be found not in the capacities of those who wield authority, nor in the symbols and rituals that attach to their activities. Rather, it lies in the structure of the relationship between the authorities and those to whom they issue their directives, in the readiness of the latter to comply with the preservation or moderation of their behavior sought by the former.

The UN's authority relationships can thus take several forms and be distributed along several continua, all of which can involve the modification of the behavior of those toward whom the exercise of authority is directed. One continuum distinguishes between formal and informal authority, between authority that is recorded in Security Council votes and the International Court of Justice decisions on the one hand and authoritative actions or words that are not written down but are no less effective in achieving compliance. Another continuum differentiates various forms of authority in terms of the time that elapses between its exercise and the compliance it evokes, with one extreme requiring immediate compliance and the other not being specific as to when a compliant action is expected. Still another focuses on the difference between authority that evokes compliance and authority that is not confirmed through a compliant response but at the same time is not rejected and is thus inferentially accepted. Equally important, there is the distinction between authority that is effective because its targets comply and authority that is effective because third parties do not object to it being exercised against the targets. As will be seen, Chinese abstentions in the Security Council's votes on the use of force against Iraq are clear-cut examples of this latter form of authority.

It follows that the UN's authority to get a member state to undertake or to desist from a course of action is not the only basis for determining its extent and effectiveness. Its agencies can exercise authority in a variety of ways that are so habitual that both member states and observers come to take it for granted. Consider, for example, this listing of activities that occur without evoking controversy over their authoritative foundations: "UN agencies set agendas; determine rules and procedures to be followed in reaching decisions beyond what is specified in the constitutional instruments; create subordinate organs, commissions, committees, inquiry missions, and panels of various kinds and fix their terms of reference; organize international conferences and decide where they meet; establish the principles and guidelines to be followed in employing secretariat members; choose executive heads; elect members of organs and subsidiary bodies and name officers of plenary and other bodies; and alter constitutional instruments."[40]

Thus far the analysis is as applicable to the period preceding the onset of turbulence as it is to the present era. How, then, might the transformation of the three parameters affect the UN's authority? In part, we have outlined an answer to the question in the aforenoted interpretation that the bifurcation of global structures has enabled the UN to augment its autonomy in the multi-centric world. It seems clear that the more autonomous the UN is in addressing the social and economic problems of actors in this world, the more likely it is to enlarge its authority in these spheres. That is, as states and sovereignty-free actors become increasingly accustomed to UN agencies acting autonomously in nonmilitary issue areas, the more likely they are to accord ever greater legitimacy and authority to such actions. More accurately, as noted below, this attribution of legitimacy is likely to be made as long as the performances of UN agencies are within the framework of acceptable criteria.

But there remains the war-and-peace realm where the sovereignty principle is deeply ensconced in the state-centric world. How might the advent of turbulence affect the UN's authority in this issue area? The answer involves a multiplicity of factors and complex processes of interaction. As the density and dynamism of world politics continue to expand, a growing awareness of the in-effectiveness of war as an instrument of national policy, as well as a deepening revulsion with respect to its horrors, has evolved.[41] More capable of appreciating that the aftermath of war can be as plagued with as many problems as the resort to military action was designed to solve, people everywhere are increasingly resistant to policies that can culminate in the onset of prolonged combat. To be sure, the world is not free of ideologues and jingoist war-mongers, but the greater analytic skills of citizens, the advent of global television that brings the realities of war into the home, and the correlative evolution of a worldwide norm surrounding the values associated with human rights and dignity seem to have led to a pervasive war-weariness, to reluctant publics and invigorated peace movements.

It is possible, of course, to cite exceptions, such as the Iraqi attack on Kuwait and the subsequent response of the thirty-one-nation coalition led by the United States, in which the use of force was widely considered appropriate. Yet, no matter how violent and extensive these exceptions may seem, it is questionable whether they express a central tendency inasmuch as their apparent appropriateness derives largely from the fact that war-weariness could not set in because the military operations lasted only several weeks. Indeed, the present period provides a more conspicuous tendency indicative of the growing awareness of the ineffectiveness of war: it was not sheer coincidence that six wars came to an end in 1988,[42] or at least the simultaneity of these similar outcomes strongly suggests how the transformation of global parameters has impacted on the viability of war as a tool of statecraft.[43]

If pervasive public doubts about the wisdom of resorting to military action are pondered in the context of states whose authority has been weakened and whose officials are thus more hesitant about the readiness of their citizenries to make the commitments necessary to wage successful wars, it seems reasonable to presume that new opportunities are developing for the UN in the war-peace realm. This may be especially the case when wars begin with overt and unmistakable attacks that cross national boundaries. Unlike conflicts initiated through terrorism and infiltrated guerrilla movements, wars that start with the conventional movement of troops across borders evoke all the emotions that attach to the sovereignty principle as well as those associated with war-weariness. Thus, it is hardly surprising that the two occasions when the UN Security Council authorized a resort to military action, in Korea in 1950 and Iraq in 1991, were both distinguished by the overtness of their beginnings. The capacity of the United States to mobilize thirty-one states to join the UN-sponsored coalition against Iraq is also a logical consequence of the new parameter values that are sustaining turbulence in world politics. Indeed, while the commitments of the thirty-one states to the war effort varied considerably, their number is a good indication of the spreading norm that rejects the legitimacy of overt and conventional military onslaughts.

This is not to contend, however, that the world has made an about-face with respect to the sovereignty principle. Doubtless that principle still remains as a core premise in the foreign offices of the state-centric world. Indeed, in the case of many former colonial countries, the sovereignty principle is their prime asset, since virtually all of them acquired statehood without the economic and consensual foundations that sustain effective governance. For such states to allow any inroads into their sovereignty would be to diminish greatly their leverage in seeking economic and development assistance from their industrialized counterparts in the state-centric world.[44]

Nevertheless, as the Gulf War demonstrates, the inviolability of the principle has been undermined. In acknowledging that the Iraqi invasion of Kuwait was not a domestic, local, or regional problem, that it constituted a global challenge sufficient to justify collective action, state officials evidenced a readiness to ignore the sovereignty principle when collective endeavor occurs under UN sponsorship. In this respect the Chinese abstention in the voting on the Security Council resolution authorizing military action against Iraq stands out as a landmark as much as the majority vote itself. The Chinese reiterated their long-standing opposition to interference in the domestic affairs and boundary disputes of states, and yet they could not bring themselves to act on their own historic commitments. Since they could not also bring themselves to sanction what they regarded as an intrusion on the sovereignty principle, they abstained, and in that abstention one can see the balance starting to tip against the historic norms of the state-centric system pertaining to the use of force.

Some might argue that the successful intervention of the anti-Iraq coalition was due to special circumstances and therefore cannot properly be interpreted as part of a movement away from the sovereignty principle. Such an argument, however, is negated by subsequent developments: the end of the Iraq war offered even more impressive signs that turbulence has thrown the equilibrium surrounding the sovereignty principle into disequilibrium and thereby opened the door wider for the UN in the war-peace realm. Confronted with hundreds of thousands of Iraqi Kurds and Shiite Muslim Arabs fleeing Saddam Hussein's brutal repression at the war's end, the horrors of which were captured and repeatedly displayed over global television, the UN Security Council approved Resolution 688, which condemned the repression, and asked the Secretary General to investigate the plight of the refugees. The Council dismissed Iraq's objection that its handling of the problem was an internal affair and that any UN action was "blatant interference," asserting instead that the wave of refugees flowing toward Turkey and Iran threatened "international peace and security." This action was not merely an extension of the peacekeeping obligations that the UN took on at the end of the war. On the contrary, it was an entirely new intrusion into the sovereignty principle.

Once again, however, the breakthrough into uncharted areas of the sovereignty principle was not clear-cut and unqualified. The principle did not simply collapse. For Resolution 688 did not back the statement of concern for the refugees with action to protect them. That came from the United States, which was in large part moved by European pressures and by the television scenes of human suffering to undertake to establish, supply, and protect sanctuary sites for Kurdish refugees in northern Iraq. The United States contended that the building of sanctuaries came under Resolution 688, but Secretary General Javier Pérez de Cuéllar questioned whether the United States could lawfully intervene on Iraqi soil without a new and explicit authorization by the Security Council. When the United States subsequently sought approval for a United Nations police force to replace its forces in northern Iraq, the Secretary General sent an envoy to Baghdad to ask for Iraq's approval of the idea. Iraq rejected the request, claiming it involved an illegal violation of Iraqi sovereignty, and the Secretary General reiterated that new Security Council authorization was needed for the UN to take over the policing process. The United States was reported not to have sought the new authority on the grounds that both the Soviet Union and China opposed UN intervention without Iraq's consent. Their opposition had its roots in the multi-centric world, with the Chinese being fearful that the Tibetans could theoretically appeal for the same sort of UN protection and the Soviets having the same fear with respect to the Baltic republics.

So the tipping of the balance against the sovereignty principle has been halting and spasmodic. But it has tipped. The global preoccupation with human rights provides ample and continuing evidence of the shifting balance. And so, more recently, does the absence of a worldwide outcry in defense of the sovereignty principle and in opposition to the United States' actions in northern Iraq. Quite to the contrary: the UN's inaction on the issue was the focus of considerable criticism, with more than a few editorials and columnists praising the United States for its compassionate actions and denouncing the UN for being mired in the sovereignty principle.[45] Humanitarian imperatives, many argued, take precedence over those affirming nonintervention, thus justifying relaxation of the sovereignty principle. While this argument has yet to be given expression through action resolutions by the Security Council, the fact that it has been vigorously advanced in the multi-centric world—and reinforced by television pictures of unspeakable horror—suggests that the pressure on the UN to supplement its words with action on such matters is likely to build in the future.[46] If it is the case that the world's concern for human rights is expanding, surely it will not be long before a worldwide preoccupation with human dignity takes root.

There is, moreover, the fact that the circumstances surrounding the ouster of Iraq from Kuwait and the subsequent response to the plight of the Kurds is part of the memory bank on which actors in both worlds of world politics will draw in the future. The incremental expansion of the authority of the UN may not have been clearly established by the Gulf War and its aftermath, but neither has it been reversed. An increment did occur and, as such, it fits well into the aforementioned trendline, the same pattern that has lately led to the UN supervising national elections in Nicaragua and Haiti—to mention only two of the more salient instances where "the work of humanitarian organizations is pushing forward the ethics and logic of the right to intervene."[47] They are part of what one observer depicts as "a sequence of episodes involving conflict and its abatement through the UN [that can] be expected to make actors aware of the fact that they are subject to constraints other than their relative weakness vis-à-vis their opponents. Such constraints include the need to justify themselves when attacked in a UN forum, to be threatened with boycotts or ostracism, to be made the subject of peacekeeping against their will. The constraints also include the recognition that persistence in unilateral behavior can result in eventual isolation and even defeat."[48] In other words, the threat of opprobrium matters as states become increasingly sensitive to humanitarian considerations. In an age where citizens are more analytically skillful and more ready to render judgments founded on performance criteria, the more governments are subject to caring about their international esteem and the reactions of publics at home.

THE POTENTIAL OF PERFORMANCE CRITERIA

Inasmuch as the UN is an actor on the global stage, presumably it is as affected by the shift from traditional to performance criteria of legitimacy as are states, public officials, and private organizations. Yet, anticipating and tracing the impact of the shift on the UN is more difficult than in the other cases. The problem arises out of the UN's seemingly amorphous identity. It is at one and the same time an international actor, a vehicle for international actors, and a site at which interaction occurs among international actors. Unfortunately, it is all too easy to lose sight of these distinctions and attribute competence to a vague and unspecified entity that is merely a locale, a collection of buildings in which activities unfold. Here, however, the UN is conceived exclusively as an actor, as a collectivity greater than the sum of its members in the sense that agencies and officials act in its name.

Unlike states, governments, and actors in the multi-centric world, the UN is not readily linked to a single leader, administration, or territorial location. Rather, it is a widely dispersed system, the actions of which are embodied in the resolutions of its Security Council and General Assembly as well as in the numerous agencies that implement its policies. None of these move around on the global stage in such a way as to be easily recognized or easily held accountable. To be sure, at any moment in time the UN's Secretary General gives voice to its aspirations, problems, and plans, but the voice of the Secretary General is widely heard more as that of a legislative spokesperson who cautiously articulates the minimal area of agreement possible within a diverse and conflicted legislature than as that of a decisive executive who speaks authoritatively for his organization.

In short, it is by no means clear whose performances are involved, or of what concrete actions they consist, when people undertake to apply criteria for evaluating how well the UN is doing in any given situation. The widespread notion that "there is no United Nations other than the collectivity of member governments"[49] can serve to disperse responsibility so extensively as to paralyze assessment. On the other hand, the very image of the UN's amorphous and dispersed structure puts it in a position of being evaluated positively when a situation turns out well and not being blamed when things go astray. That is, if circumstances are seen as having been improved, or at least not worsened, by virtue of the UN's actions, then it will be viewed as having met appropriate standards of performance. But if the circumstances are considered to have worsened, or if they are regarded as a reflection of failure, then the UN's contribution can be excused on the grounds that its efforts were hindered by the sovereignty principle.

This tendency to exonerate the UN is further reinforced by the authority crises that have beset states. Inclined to fault either their own or other governments for the persistence of intractable problems, people are less likely to focus their doubts and criticisms on the UN.[50]

This is not to ignore the fact that the UN's history records moments when its performances, especially votes in the Security Council and General Assembly, have been criticized, even condemned, by those whose interests were offended. Israel's annoyance over the 1974 General Assembly resolution equating Zionism with racism and Third World antagonism to the thwarting of its demands for new information and economic orders are perhaps the most conspicuous examples in this regard. Indeed, these resentments have tended to linger and reinforce the perception of biased majorities as international actors. On the other hand, one wonders how long the perception of a collective bias will survive in the event of offsetting performances in specific situations. Israel may long give voice to a distaste for UN involvement in Middle East affairs, and some Third World countries may long object to the dominance of First World concerns in UN deliberations; but it is possible to imagine a shift in these orientations if concrete performances by the Secretary General or other organs begin to convey alternative perspectives.

On balance, then, it seems reasonable to conclude that the UN benefits from the shifting criteria of performance. As people become increasingly performance-oriented and as they increasingly come to question the competence of states, the UN seems destined to gain. Its legitimacy is bound to undergo incremental enrichment as it becomes ever more enmeshed in the two worlds of world politics and enjoys successes that are increasingly assessed in terms of what happens rather than in terms of traditional criteria that delineate what forms of action are constitutionally or politically appropriate.

In an important sense the tendency to question the performance of states is why the UN has survived for so long. The crises and setbacks that marked the first forty-five years of its existence were attributed to the superpowers, to the veto power of the five permanent members of the Security Council, and to the sovereignty principle, thus diverting attention from the UN and enabling it to persist and mature as an institution. If the League of Nations came to an end because of a world war it could not prevent, the UN has endured because such a war never occurred and because it has not been held responsible for intervening crises.

It might be argued that this estimate of the impact of performance criteria of legitimacy suffers from the fact that only a small proportion of the world's peoples have had occasion to observe the UN in action. So much of the UN's work is rooted in studies and conferences, this line of reasoning asserts, that only the tip of the iceberg is available for evaluation. Unlike states, whose agents interface with citizens in a great variety of ways, UN personnel are posted at distant trouble spots and thus not visible to most people. Or, to the extent the work of the UN is readily open to assessment by large populations, it is when the deliberations of its General Assembly and Security Council are televised, circumstances that only demonstrate what a sovereignty-bound, dispersed organization it is and thus not conducive to the application of performance criteria. How, then, the argument concludes, can the UN possibly be the focus of favorable evaluations?

While there is no doubt that the UN could benefit from more effective efforts to inform and educate publics about its diverse endeavors, the contention that it is essentially an invisible presence in world politics is flawed for several reasons. One is that one or another of its agencies has been drawn into many of the situations fostered by the onset of turbulence. From elections in divided polities to humanitarian work in Africa, from peacekeeping in Lebanon to peacemaking in the Iran-Iraq war, from development activities in Asia to peace enforcement in Kuwait, from formulating a code for the marketing of baby foods to focusing year-long attention on the deterioration of the environment or the plight of children, the UN system is much more salient than it was in earlier eras. Indeed, the headquarters of its agencies are located in thirty-four countries, and a recent perusal of its phone book lists cable connections to offices in 117 cities throughout the world.[51]

Second, there appears to be an increasing number and variety of situations where the UN is viewed as a highly relevant actor. Most notably perhaps, the Bush administration was impelled to get the approval of the Security Council at crucial stages in the campaign to oust Iraq from Kuwait. Hardly less conspicuous is the large extent to which actors in the Third World turn to the UN as a means of contesting the dominance of the First World. As previously indicated, their inclinations to perceive the UN as having compiled a history of articulating First World interests can be offset by a recognition of the large extent to which their majority in the General

Assembly has protected and advanced their interests. The insistence of several Third World countries that the UN be involved in sponsoring a conference on Arab-Israeli tensions after the Gulf War is a recent instance of a readiness to turn to the UN as a mechanism for addressing and resolving conflict situations.

Third, it is too simple to proceed from the assumption that "whatever the United Nations says or does . . . reflects the collective decisions of its member governments."[52] This may be so in a variety of ways, but it is also the case that, like any collectivity, the whole is larger than the sum of its parts, that the aggregation of its members' inputs creates an entity that "says" and "does" outputs that stand on their own, apart from those who contributed to their formulation.[53] Concrete evidence of the UN's separateness as an identifiable actor in world politics can be seen in the fact that it has a legal standing, constitutional bases, organizational precedents, a flag, property, bank accounts, and institutionally committed executive heads and staffs. For all its lack of publicity, in short, the UN would appear to occupy much more of a spotlight on the world stage than it ever has previously.

THE CONSEQUENCES OF MORE ANALYTICALLY SKILLFUL CITIZENS

Since the UN is composed of states rather than people and thus lacks the kind of constituencies that governments and subnational organizations have, it might seem far-fetched to probe its operations for consequences of the worldwide impact of expanding analytic skills. Yet, the impact of this dimension of global turbulence cannot be discounted. It may not directly impact on the UN because individuals tend to look to their governments for the framing of suitable policies or the redressing of noxious wrongs, but there are a number of indirect routes through which the expanded competence of individuals can be traced. Foremost among these, of course, are the pressures that publics exert on their own governments to extend, contract, or otherwise sustain their relationships to the UN—to pay the assessed dues, to comply with UN resolutions, to provide the resources and personnel needed for peacekeeping operations, to intensify or downplay criticism of the Secretary General, and to cast or reverse particular votes in the legislative arenas of the UN. Such pressures are not irrelevant to the context within which the UN seeks to advance its collective goals. The votes its members' delegates cast, the decisions of the Secretary General, and the day-to-day field operations of its agencies are all partially responsive to the climate of opinion that prevails at a given moment in time with respect to the general esteem in which the UN is held. To be sure, publics are fickle and their moods can swing widely for and against the UN. But it is reasonable to presume that as people become more analytically skillful, as they become more and more appreciative of the complexity of world affairs, and as they become more sensitive to the limits within which their governments must operate, the fluctuations in their moods are likely to diminish and their grasp of the roles the UN can play is likely to deepen.

This is not to imply that the UN may become a focus of loyalties. Quite to the contrary: the prospects for the tendencies toward centralization in world politics resulting in the UN emerging as the focus for the loyalties of people seem very remote indeed. Some day there may be a world government, and the UN may some day be that world government, but the bifurcation of world politics is too hospitable to the sovereignty principle to imagine a time in the near future when the UN replaces states as a primary focus of primary loyalties. On the other hand, the foregoing is to say that individuals are not so wedded to the sovereignty principle that they are unable to lift their sights beyond the nation-state and attach significance to supranational actors. Just as the tendency to assess negatively the performance of states leads people to search for subnational actors that can more effectively address their problems, so are they likely to be drawn to IOs that can serve their needs or values. Amnesty International, for example, appears to command the loyalty of a large and voluntary membership that responds to appeals for practical actions as well as financial donations.

An indication that citizens can raise their sights to the supranational level is provided by the participation of European voters in the three elections that have been held for the European Parliament. In 1979, 1984, and 1989 the turnout rates were, respectively, 62, 60, and 57 percent, figures that are especially impressive when it is appreciated that these were legislative elections that could not result in the selection of a chief executive. Indeed, all three percentages exceed the proportion of those who vote in US presidential elections, and they far exceed the proportion of Americans who participate in off-year elections for the Congress. Likewise, it seems reasonable to anticipate that more analytically skillful citizenries will become increasingly capable of discerning that the UN is more than the sum of its parts, that its activities can ameliorate problems and serve useful functions, that its support offers them a degree of legitimacy, that it offers means for networking with counterparts elsewhere in the world, and that there are situations in which its efforts may be more effective than any that governments can undertake. It may be more than a mere mood fluctuation, for example, that the American people, after years of negative orientations toward the UN, were recently found to favor by a 4-to-1 margin the idea that all its member states, including the United States, should provide more tax money, not less, for peacekeeping forces."[54] Equally noteworthy, after the Gulf War the performance orientations of the American people were such that in one poll 70 percent said they had gained respect for the UN, while only 4 percent lost respect.[55] In still another poll an even higher 85 percent said they preferred that the UN rather than the United States take the lead in combating future aggression.[56]

Furthermore, in those numerous crisis situations where the UN's presence is unmistakable, the enhanced analytic skills of those involved surely facilitate the prospect for favorable outcomes. Such skills enabled people in Nambia, Haiti, and Nicaragua to feel free to turn out and vote in fair elections. They enabled Greeks and Turks in Cyprus to maintain their fragile peace by respecting the UN peacekeeping forces that separated them. They facilitated the readiness of Kurds in northern Iraq to come out of the hills and settle into refugee camps flying the UN flag. These are only a few of the situations where the work of the UN appears to have been strengthened by enhanced skills that allowed people to break out of their national or subnational habits and perceive the UN as also capable of serving their welfare.

Nor is there any reason to believe that those who have had direct contacts with the UN have become blind to its limits or naive about its potential. On the contrary, the skill revolution includes a capacity to appreciate the relevance of power to the structure of situations and thus to recognize that a key element of many situations involves the sovereignty principle and the pitting of the UN's moral authority against the military competence of states. In the case of the Kurds' return to northern Iraq, for example, the presence of US armed forces was perceived as crucial to their security from attacks by Saddam Hussein's armies. "If American troops are here [in Dohuk], the people can come home," a 36-year-old driver, Ahmed Youssef, was quoted as observing. "If not, then they will not come. The United Nations is terrific, but the protection of the Americans is better." But such an attitude does not tell the whole story. UN security guards were also brought to Dohuk and made "very visible"—in white Land Rovers flying the UN flag, with UN emblems on their uniforms—as a means of reassuring people and thereby swelling the flow of returnees. To be sure, the flow grew because word of the US presence spread and because Kurdish leaders worked out an agreement on regional autonomy with Baghdad; but surely it is also a measure of enhanced analytic skills, the relocation of authority, and the relevance of performance criteria of legitimacy that the slow return of the refugees accompanied the arrival of UN officials making much of their presence.[57]

Put differently, the advent of turbulence in world politics has led to the UN supplementing, not replacing, other dynamics that may be at work in present-day conflicts. The role of the UN in current situations may not be predominant; but as a consequence of the transformation of the basic parameters of world politics, neither is its role trivial. World politics derive from multiple sources, and increasingly the UN is one of those sources.

THE IMPACT OF SUBGROUPISM

As subgroups become more numerous, coherent, and sensitive about their autonomous identity, and especially as many of them are thus led into interethnic and intercommunal conflict, the demands for the involvement of UN agencies in the internal affairs of states seem likely to grow. Recent conflicts in Afghanistan, Angola, Chad, Grenada, Haiti, and Nicaragua, for example, were pervaded with international dimensions, but at base they sprung from domestic conflicts, a fact that did not prevent a turn to the UN for peacemaking and peacekeeping assistance. Indeed, the very participation of the UN in such a wide array of internal conflict situations is testimony to the large extent to which the transformations wrought by turbulence have swept away the boundaries that allegedly divide domestic from foreign affairs. Put differently, the mushrooming of subgroupism, of decentralizing tendencies that undermine the authority of states and fragment the ties of societies, has added immensely to the workload of the UN. Often feeling isolated within their historical locales, subgroups tend to reach out for all kinds of assistance from abroad the more embattled they are at home, a process that often leads them to the doorstep of the UN where, they feel, legitimacy and support for their aspirations can be found.

If the UN's workload grows as a consequence of rampant subgroupism, so of course will the aforenoted vacuum that lies between the sovereignty principle of the state-centric world and the autonomy principle of the multi-centric world. It seems likely, therefore, that top UN officials will be increasingly faced with the choice of expanding the organization's presence in the domestic affairs of states. Given a solidification of the emergent parameters of world politics, one can readily envision this process cumulating to the point where certain kinds of UN interventions, such as those involving contested elections and refugee flows (if not pending or actual internal wars), become commonplace and institutionalized. The extension of such patterns will, in turn, focus the spotlight of performance criteria ever more brightly on the way in which UN agencies shoulder these responsibilities.

In sum, there is a whole range of reasons to conclude that the transformations at work in world politics are enlarging, and will continue to enlarge, the UN's centrality in the emergent global order. If the UN has been relegated to the sidelines for more than four decades because states have been reluctant to acknowledge its utility and potential, the conditions of world politics today allow for the UN to enter vigorously onto the field of play. As its roles expand and become increasingly institutionalized, the opportunities for the UN to move beyond adapting to change and to serve also as an agent of change seem bound to multiply. This expectation highlights a vital policy question to which this analysis now turns: What can be done to maximize the UN's chances of functioning as an agent of positive rather than negative change?

5

THE UN AS AN
AGENT OF CHANGE

It is possible to conceive of the UN as performing important functions in world politics without presuming that it operates as an important source of change. World affairs might not be the same today, and they might even be much worse, if the UN had not been established in 1945. But to perform key functions that make a difference is not necessarily to operate as an agent of change. During this period the UN's activities may have occurred largely as a consequence of the changes rather than as a producer of them. A balanced view of the UN's record in this regard, however, suggests otherwise. While the organization has in many instances merely reflected the changes that have marked the decades since World War II, there are at the same time more than a few changes that can be traced in some measure to the deliberations of UN agencies, votes in the General Assembly, and actions of the Secretary General. Most notably perhaps, much of the historic postwar move to end colonialism and the subsequent stress on the preservation and promotion of human rights can be traced to the debates and actions of the UN. Similarly, a wide array of UN decisions and actions in the ecological field during the 1970s helped transform the way in which environmental problems were viewed by national governments and raised high on the agendas of communities. Indeed, the spreading awareness of a deep and worldwide interdependence linking humankind to planetary conditions—what has been called the "global problematique"—can readily be attributed to a series of developments that occurred under UN sponsorship.[58]

To speak of the UN as a change agent is not to refer to a uniform process or particular actors in the organization. There are a variety of ways in which diverse UN agencies can foster change in different issue areas. In the environmental field, for example, the

59

transformations had their origin in the leadership of a coalition of northern European and moderate Third World countries in the General Assembly and other UN deliberative bodies,[59] whereas the changes brought about in the peacekeeping realm were due, at least in part, to the work of the Secretary General and his subordinates in the UN Secretariat.[60]

Nor, it must be quickly added, is the ensuing analysis of the UN's potential as a change agent meant to imply that it is capable of bringing about huge changes that will fundamentally alter the course of events. Sizable transformations are the product of many factors, and while the UN may be one factor, it would be erroneous to tease out its contribution and treat it as the sole source of change. Accordingly, the discussion highlights noticeable but nonetheless modest changes, shifts in attitudes that are discernible alterations rather than wholesale reversals, trendlines that reflect gentle upward slopes rather than steep curves, and cumulative processes that are incremental rather than revolutionary.[61] What follows, in short, focuses on the potential for marginal changes that may well add up to significant transformations with the passage of time.

The reference, moreover, is to long stretches of time—to years and not weeks—that are sufficient to allow for the surfacing of trendlines. Such a time perspective takes the analysis beyond the success or failure of particular undertakings. Trendlines are composed of both, of jagged edges that move erratically in one direction if viewed across enough incidents to allow for a pattern to emerge despite the peaks and valleys. The ensuing analysis, in other words, does not deny that UN efforts are susceptible to failure. At least four types of past failures have been identified—ranging from destabilizing policies that discourage long-term solutions to those that intensify short-term disputes—and there is no reason to believe they will not occur again in the future and result in unwanted negative effects.[62] Whatever may be the setbacks and disappointments, however, the search here is for potential ways in which the UN can contribute as a change agent to central tendencies that depict positive and stabilizing patterns.

Most analyses of what the UN can accomplish focus on its internal decisionmaking procedures rather than on those points in the emergent structures of world politics that are vulnerable to its influence. Here, temptations to focus on organizational tinkerings that might improve the UN's work are resisted in favor of six policy recommendations that will enable it to seize the opportunities opened up by the onset of turbulence and the parametric transformations that have followed. In so doing, mention is made of the need to streamline and improve the UN's policymaking processes, but it must nevertheless be stressed that the ensuing proposals have been generated by the analysis of global structures and how they may enable the UN to induce change, rather than by a close examination of the UN's internal workings.

Finally, what follows does not presume a zero-sum game in which the UN and nation-states are locked into an antagonistic contest that can result in only one of them winning. As has always been the case, challenges cannot be met and changes cannot be initiated if only single actors undertake such tasks. The world's problems lend themselves to nonzero-sum solutions in which the UN, national governments, and other agents of change collaborate in such a way that all concerned benefit from any positive outcomes that may be accomplished. Our focus is on the UN's contribution to such outcomes, but the policy recommendations set forth below do not preclude the cooperation of other actors. Indeed, their central thrust is on activities that will persuade the member states of the UN to approve, or otherwise to accept, steps that would enhance the authority and effectiveness of IOs in coping with the changes and challenges that lie ahead.

RECOMMENDATION 1:
TOWARD ATTITUDINAL CHANGE

As previously implied, the sovereignty principle is not an absolute. It is, rather, a mental construction that has been expressed through constitutional instruments, historical precedents, and political actions. As such, as an expression of deeply held, unquestioned values about the structure of human affairs in the modern period, the sovereignty principle has become a given in the minds of leaders and publics as they interpret the UN Charter, subsequent General Assembly and Security Council decisions, and the international conduct of states. Nevertheless, despite its seemingly absolute quality, the sovereignty principle is subject to reinterpretation, modification, and revision if circumstances in world affairs change sufficiently to make the unquestionable begin to seem questionable.

It follows that if the foregoing assessment is correct—that large transformations have accompanied the onset of turbulence in world politics—leaders and publics can be expected to become increasingly open to reinterpreting the sovereignty principle, to approaching all the documents and actions that underlie UN policies and practices in a new context that is not limited by any dogma. Accordingly, it is recommended that stress be placed on the virtues of a new mind-set relative to the sovereignty principle; that public officials, leaders in the private sector, and citizens be encouraged to ponder a reconstruction of the principle such that it is viewed as subject to more than one interpretation; that there are broad as well as narrow conceptions of sovereignty; and that none of the various conceptions lies beyond the pale of modification.

Inducing such attitudinal reorientations can well begin by emphasizing that while the sovereignty principle has been interpreted for forty years as favoring the rights of states vis-à-vis IOs as collective actors, this does not mean that the balance must forever be tipped so fully and forcefully in this direction. Like the Cold War, which collapsed in no time at all because it was sustained by obsolete pictures of international structure that leaders and publics carried around in their heads, the sovereignty principle can be portrayed as susceptible to swift revision if the attitudes that sustain it are felt to be approaching obsolescence.

Given the advent of a bifurcated global structure, the proliferation of authority crises, the decreasing ability of states to cope with challenges originating both at home and abroad, and the greater skills of citizens everywhere, this would seem to be an especially propitious moment in world history to develop and pursue a new mind-set with respect to the sovereignty principle. The uncertainties of world politics are now so pervasive that a concerted effort to emphasize the inherent flexibility of the principle, to stress the broad range within which it can be reinterpreted without being rejected, may well help shape the nature of the emergent global order and the roles the UN can play in it.

To facilitate stress on the flexibility of the sovereignty principle, an empirical inquiry could usefully be launched into the extent to which the new mind-set has already begun to evolve. With the onset of turbulence having given pause to many people, it may well be that the erosion of the sovereignty principle is greater than appears to be the case impressionistically. If so, a systematic study of this possibility could be used to hasten the evolutionary process.

Whatever such a research project might yield, the effort to nurse the development of new political orientations should obviously not imply that the sovereignty principle needs to be abandoned. To appear to be arguing for the replacement of states with some form of world government would surely evoke resistance and rejection. Rather, the focus should be on the limits that confront states in the face of global turbulence, on the great variety of ways in which governments are caught up in a confluence of dynamics that are new and that perforce compel them to be readier to equate their national interests with those of the larger global community. The dictates of history, it can now be easily asserted, are propelling humankind toward a new global order in which choices no longer need to be made in terms of values that posit states as ensconced in a vast zero-sum game.

Note that the desired attitudinal changes do not focus on the UN. Progress toward new perspectives would not be measured by the degree to which the UN is upgraded. On the contrary, the implications for the role of the UN need not be flagged. They would follow once the sovereignty principle was seen as flexible and subject to revision. More accurately, once such a flexibility becomes operative, the work of the UN would be seen less in a convenience-of-the-states context and more in a states-sometimes-are-obliged-to-go-along context.

Evolution of the recommended attitudes would be sought on the part of all UN officials whose responsibilities allow and require them to articulate actions that may be appropriate for the organization to undertake. Most notably, it is a modified mind-set that the Secretary General and his top aides in the Secretariat need to bring into their negotiations with the representatives of national governments. This will not be easy for personnel who have long been accustomed to interpreting the sovereignty principle in favor of the member states. For them now to give voice to a perspective that calls on states to yield some of their jurisdiction in certain issue areas is to ask them to quell deep-seated habits and to be less deferential in requesting cooperation. They will need to evolve an appreciation of the extent of the changes that have undermined the sovereignty principle and to be ready to take advantage of the new circumstances by contesting counterarguments they used to accept. Put differently, where they once saw themselves as diplomatic in their readiness to acquiesce to representatives of national governments, now they will have to define themselves as accomplished diplomats when they use reason and tact to persuade the same officials to be more flexible in their application of the sovereignty principle. Admittedly, some of those who lead the Secretariat may not succeed in making an appropriate attitudinal shift, which is why it is recommended below that flexibility along this attitudinal dimension be made a crucial criterion in the future recruitment of persons to fill the UN's leadership positions.

Clearly, however, the revised predispositions toward the sovereignty principle must extend well beyond officials high in the

UN's structure. Administrative policies also need to be developed that will lead to the inculcation of a revised orientation toward national sovereignty on the part of those in the field responsible for carrying out the peacekeeping and other day-to-day tasks of the UN. Attitudinal movement along these lines by field personnel will also serve to add to their sense of mission as they begin to sense they are on the cutting edge of a large change in their organization's place in world politics.

Nor should efforts to promote the new states-sometimes-are-obliged-to-go-along interpretation of the sovereignty principle be confined to those on the UN's payroll. Such efforts should also be pursued among leaders in both the state-centric and multi-centric worlds, with the UN's involvement in the Gulf War and the subsequent creation of safety zones for Kurdish refugees in northern Iraq being cited often as precedents for a revised view of the delicate balance on which the sovereignty principle rests. Again, resistance to this new way of thinking will surely be considerable in foreign offices and those private centers where the prerogatives of national sovereignty are given top priority. But if journalists, television commentators, party chiefs, educators, the clergy, business executives, labor leaders, and others who are able to circulate their perspectives widely are persuaded to introduce nuance into their presumptions about the nature of sovereignty in today's world, it should be possible to initiate a momentum that redefines the place of the UN and the way in which its performances are assessed. The momentum toward redefinition may move slowly, but if the end of the Cold War is any indication, it could well accelerate at an ever more rapid rate.

In order to sustain and quicken the momentum toward attitudinal change, a number of small steps could be taken that may have significant consequences. Extensive lists could be compiled, for example, of historical situations where a slightly different, nonthreatening interpretation of the sovereignty principle could have altered outcomes. Hypothetical scenarios could also be constructed that demonstrate both the flexibility of the principle and the beneficial consequences that can flow from not treating it as an absolute. In short, while this is not the place to outline the kind of educational program that could be launched on behalf of new attitudes toward the balance between the rights of states and transnational requirements, there would seem to be no lack of schemes that could be implemented to seize this propitious moment for rethinking the limits of sovereignty in a world racked by turbulence.

RECOMMENDATION 2:
TOWARD ENHANCED AUTHORITY

While the enhancement of legitimacy in world politics has become closely tied to the adequacy of performances, obviously the performances must be readily observable if their quality is to be evaluated. If much of the work of the UN involves routinized activities unheralded by the mass media, there is little likelihood that its performances will be observed sufficiently for authority to be relocated in the direction of its policies and activities. Citizens may have increasingly refined skills for evaluating UN performances, but they can hardly be expected to exercise them if the organization's personnel and activities are inconspicuous except on those rare moments of crisis when events move them to front and center on the world stage. How, then, to take advantage of the uncertainties precipitated by global turbulence to enhance the probability of the UN acquiring greater authority by making its presence more visible and salient for people everywhere? In particular, how to enhance the UN's visibility in those instances when it engages in peacekeeping and other forms of preventive maintenance that constrain conflicts from escalating into violence, i.e., in those instances when the UN is both most successful and least visible?

While many answers to these questions could doubtless be developed, here the recommendation is that every member of the UN be asked to donate property in its capital for the establishment of a permanent UN mission on its soil. The missions would not be called embassies or consulates because the intention is to make their services available to people and organizations in the multi-centric world as well as to the host governments. To prevent each mission from becoming too immersed in the affairs of the state-centric world, its personnel, tasks, and operating funds would be provided by the Secretariat in New York, which would also monitor its work and receive its reports. Each country would pay an annual tax to the UN for the services provided by the mission on its territory.

The services offered by each mission would include information about its peacekeeping activities and the work of its various technical agencies of the UN, conferences relevant to the UN's programs in the host country, opportunities for employment in the UN system, educational and research materials produced by UNESCO and other agencies, and whatever special activities may be upcoming on the UN's agenda. In addition, each mission would be expected to sponsor lectures, art shows, and other presentations expressive of its activities throughout the world. The UN flag would fly alongside that of the host country at a conspicuous place on the mission property, atop its building or from a flagpole on the grounds. A minimal security guard, wearing UN uniforms, would protect the mission from vandalism.

Much as is the case for embassies and consulates, country mission doors would be open to all those who had occasion to turn to one or another UN agency for assistance. The host government might try to attempt to keep certain of its citizens—such as leaders of opposition parties—from visiting the mission, but the principle would be immediately established that all citizens and groups would be equally entitled to access to the mission. If the number of persons seeking access was excessively high, it would be the mission and not the host government that would determine the schedule through which access was provided. If the solicitations for assistance by the mission exceeded its competence or jurisdiction, it would advise those seeking admission to its offices where they would have to go to obtain the desired help.

As previously noted, to some extent a network of offices of various UN agencies does exist in some national capitals. While these have functional assignments and are not diplomatic missions in the sense being proposed here, they often do perform some of the reporting and representing tasks of traditional diplomacy. Where there are resident representatives of the UN Development Programme, such officials may be charged with coordinating the work of the various UN personnel in that country. In addition, some of the UN's offices abroad fly the UN flag and are guarded by uniformed UN personnel. Still, this network is uneven and does not extend to all the members of the UN. Equally important, the functional offices do not enjoy the kind of status envisioned for the formal country missions that would be established under this proposal. Presumably the network of existing functional offices would be absorbed into the formal missions of the relevant countries once the latter were established.

There is, of course, no guarantee that a network of permanent UN missions located around the world would enhance the organization's authority. As previously noted, some countries go through periods of regarding the UN as strongly biased against them—as Iran did because of the Security Council's failure to condemn Iraq for starting the war against it in 1980, or as the United States did during the Reagan years when the majority in the General Assembly was arrayed solidly against many US policies, or as Israel has continued to do since the General Assembly passed a resolution in 1975 equating Zionism with racism. Any trend toward endowing the UN with more authority is likely to be halting at best, and even in countries with favorable inclinations toward the UN, the trend is unlikely to trace more than a gentle upward slope. Given the historical commitments of the state-centric world, that is, the greater institutional presence of the UN is bound to stimulate resistance and counterpressures. Some countries may not want the UN's presence among them enhanced. Others will say they are unable to bear the costs involved, and some of these may in fact be unable to bear them. Thus, while there are ways to offset the cost factor (see below), the establishment of UN missions in a number of countries would doubtless encounter numerous obstacles and take years to reach fruition.

Nevertheless, given the dynamics underlying the authority crises that pervade world politics, in the long run the greater salience of the UN's personnel and activities would seem likely to attract attention and respect, thereby setting the conditions for a slow accretion of authority. And, assuming the organization's reputation for evenhandedness would grow through its more extensive visibility as a neutral actor committed to the improvement of the human condition, so would people and subgroups be increasingly inclined to accord legitimacy to its actions. Put more cautiously, the availability and openness of the UN's missions in the world's capitals, combined with growing doubts about the performances of the host governments, could generate tangible opportunities for the UN to enhance its reputation for evenhandedness.[63]

RECOMMENDATION 3:
STRENGTHENING BIFURCATED STRUCTURES

While there are good reasons to assume that the bifurcation of world politics is not a transitory phenomenon,[64] so can compelling arguments be made for consolidating the structures that sustain the autonomy of the multi-centric world and inhibit states from pressing for a restoration of the old and outmoded interstate system. The two worlds of world politics have emerged because the complexities and interdependencies that mark life late in the twentieth century are no longer conducive to the traditional arrangements, but the intensity of the tensions between the centralizing and decentralizing dynamics at work on a global scale are such that the emergent bifurcated structures are still fragile and subject to being overwhelmed by governments that resist their loss of authority. The UN can thus fulfill its role as a change agent by maintaining the momentum that has brought about bifurcation.

One recommendation for accomplishing this goal concerns the work of proposed UN missions throughout the world. While these must above all enhance the UN's reputation for evenhandedness by not favoring actors in the multi-centric world over the host governments, they could nevertheless perform a number of services for the various private groups and organizations that need to establish contacts elsewhere in the multi-centric world. Through its network of country missions the UN could serve as a crucial conduit for information and settings that enable sovereignty-free actors in distant parts of the world to learn of each other's existence and to share each other's expertise. One can even imagine this network facilitating the creation of new networks among disparate but like-minded organizations and groups that would not otherwise know of each other's existence. In return, it is reasonable to expect that the multinational corporations, social movements, professional societies, and other private actors that may benefit from this network-building activity could serve as a support base for the UN mission in their country when and if the host government seeks to limit or eliminate the mission's activities.

In addition to the services each mission could perform for actors in the multi-centric world, there may be a number of ways in which it could be used by UN headquarters in New York to convey information to and exert pressure on the host government relevant to political issues under consideration by the General Assembly and the Security Council. Long-established practices of working with the country's mission in New York will, of course, continue to serve as the main mechanism for exchanging information and preferences with the Secretariat, but the availability of the UN in the country's capital could offer another channel through which ideas and requests arising out of debates in New York might be brought to the attention of foreign offices. One can readily imagine the UN mission in a country and that country's foreign office evolving routines for daily or weekly interaction over matters of mutual interest. Indeed, conceivably the embassies of other countries in the host capital could seek out the UN mission located there as another channel for pressing viewpoints on the Secretariat in New York. The advent of a network of UN missions around the world, in short, could be no less valuable to actors in the state-centric world as to their counterparts in the multi-centric world.

Another, perhaps potentially more consequential recommendation for strengthening the structures of global bifurcation involves a long-standing proposal to add a people's assembly to the UN, in which the representatives would be directly elected rather than chosen by states to serve.[65] Although the idea has never generated wide enthusiasm and a number of its dimensions remain obscure (such as how electoral districts would be constituted and delegates elected), conceivably some form of it could engender support as the uncertainties of this turbulent era, the impulses of subgroupism to break free of state controls, and the power of the skill revolution become increasingly prevalent. And however the idea may be translated into a concrete proposal, a people's assembly would have the advantage of locating the processes of global bifurcation in a clear-cut institutional context. On the other hand, such a legislature might be counterproductive in the sense that it would encourage needless conflicts between the multi- and state-centric worlds. At present such conflicts tend to be confined to particular actors over particular issues, but an institutionalization of the bifurcated structure would in all likelihood give rise to circumstances that would pit the whole of both worlds against each other and thereby undermine the strong tendencies that presently foster cooperation across the boundaries that separate the two worlds.

RECOMMENDATION 4:
TOWARD THE CREATION OF A GLOBAL SERVICE

As the multi-centric world becomes more dense with relevant actors, as the variety and number of issues in the state-centric world proliferate, and as these dynamics make the UN ever more central on the global stage, there is the clear danger that the organization will be inundated by system overload. And if the analysis presented here is correct and the authority of the UN expands to the point where ever greater numbers of contested domestic elections and violence-prone internal conflicts are brought within its peacemaking and peacekeeping orbits, the susceptibility to overload is likely to reach gigantic proportions; and the situation could become even more overpowering if the recommendation for UN missions in every member state were to be adopted. The need for an expansion of the UN's personnel, in short, is likely to be acute.

How, then, to shoulder an expanding workload that can well be regarded as the price of success? Here it is recommended that the member states, working with the UN missions located in their capitals, facilitate the recruitment of volunteers whose analytic skills are tested to be substantial and who are willing to embark on a career that involves a variety of rewards, not the least being a sense of service to the global community. The UN already has a minuscule "peace corps" as well as more numerous military personnel in peacekeeping units, but the suggestion here is that the former of these services be greatly enlarged and that its tasks be expanded to cover a number of new activities. Whether these new tasks would include the military side of peacekeeping is a question that requires considerable reflection, especially as both the UN and the member states might be unwilling, for different reasons, to have an international army come into being. Aside from the military issue, however, the recruitment and funding of a volunteer service would be founded on appeals that do not take national loyalties for granted and that presume a readiness on the part of people everywhere to contribute to the emergence of a new, more humane global order. Given more analytically skillful citizens, a readiness on their part to revise their hierarchy of loyalties, and an inclination to attribute greater legitimacy to the UN as its performance record improves, it is not unlikely that a large and varied pool of applicants can be developed and continuously replenished.

RECOMMENDATION 5:
TOWARD MORE EFFECTIVE LEADERSHIP

Not only is the core of the UN's administrative apparatus legally and otherwise responsible to the state-centric system and thus somewhat insulated from the shifting parameters of world politics, but it has also become so sizable that it is subject to all the inertia and conservatism that besets any large organization. This means that the vast changes at work in the world tend to get filtered through a state-centric prism that resists the notion that profound dynamics are transforming the global landscape. UN personnel in the various field agencies are, of course, keenly aware of transformations wrought by the skill revolution, the crises of authority, and the proliferation of the multi-centric world, but the pace at which these changes get integrated into the working knowledge of those who sustain the headquarters bureaucracy in New York is anything but rapid.[66] On the East River the sovereignty principle predominates in a variety of ways, from the staffing procedures based on regional and national quotas to the processes by which the Secretary General is selected, from the implicit premises underlying the rejection of proposals that enhance the UN's authority to the avoidance of innovative steps that might offend one or another powerful bloc.

Like any large bureaucracy, in short, the UN's is rooted into long-standing habits and cautious modes of decisionmaking. As such, as an organization prone to inertia and predisposed to do only what its member states allow it to do, restlessness over its history of caution can serve as a large reservoir of political will with which to seize the opportunities offered by the dynamics of turbulent change. Given this reservoir, it is hardly surprising that proposals to reform the Secretariat and its procedures for generating information and making decisions have become increasingly salient.

Some part of these problems will be resolved by the passage of time and the movement into top administrative posts of a new generation sensitive to the parametric transformations. The present cadre of top officials was socialized into the organization when the state-centric world was not seriously challenged and the competition of the superpowers dominated the international scene. Presumably, upcoming administrators will evolve new perspectives more attuned to the dynamics inherent in the bifurcation of world politics. Likewise, the more dense and autonomous actors in the multi-centric world become, the more will UN headquarters in New York, Geneva, Vienna, Nairobi, and elsewhere become sites of a vast lobbying arena, thus bringing the winds of change ever more fully into the upper reaches of the bureaucracy.

This is not the place to engage in a review of the proposed reforms and the obstacles they face. But an insight into the dilemma fostering more effective leadership can be developed by focusing on the position of Secretary General and the potential it offers for initiating the kind of attitudinal change that will modify the sovereignty principle and enable the UN to move more staunchly into the areas where states are excessively protective of their national interests. Although the reach of the Secretary General within the UN system does not extend to all of its agencies, many of which enjoy a great deal of autonomy, it is nonetheless the occupant of this position who infuses purpose, ideals, and overall strategies into the work of the UN. Thus it matters whether the individual who holds the post has the orientations to contest the paralyzing effects of the sovereignty principle and the bureaucratic resources to do so effectively. Secretary General Javier Pérez de Cuéllar, for example, could have gone either way with respect to whether the United States's actions in Northern Iraq fell under Resolution 688. He chose to honor the sovereignty principle and to seek a diplomatic solution in that context; but whatever the ultimate outcome of the situation, it is indicative of the many choice points where the orientations of the Secretary General, and the nature of the advice he receives from his staff, can crucially affect the course of events and the UN's adaptation to the confluence of centralizing and decentralizing tendencies.

Historically the selection of the Secretary General has been founded less on merit and more on geographic distribution, more on being a handmaiden to states and less on commitments to conflict resolution, more on traditional criteria and less on performance criteria. Thus the UN has witnessed few dramas in which strong Secretaries General are pitted against strong governments. Yet, as stressed previously, this may be an especially propitious time for such dramas to be played out, for the present and future Secretaries General to give voice to an attitude change that posits states as having to yield on the sovereignty principle and as needing to recognize they are caught up in a tide of larger forces that can only leave them isolated if they resist it.

There is no dearth of detailed recommendations on how the process of selecting future Secretaries General can be improved. Criteria for the skills required by the job, the appointment of a search committee, procedures for checking the credentials of those nominated, arrangements to avoid the principle of regional rotation in the position, and a host of other useful suggestions have been voiced that could well lead to future UN administrations that are more securely reflective of the transformations at work in world politics.[67] In none of these proposals, however, is mention made of the substantive orientations to which candidates for the job should be committed. Rather, there seems to be a pervasive presumption that the chosen candidate should be wedded to a give-states-the-benefit-of-the-doubt philosophy instead of a times-require-that-states-go-along perspective. The desired attitudinal change set forth above is conspicuous by the absence of any traces favoring it, as if all the changes that have marked the years since 1945 have no relevance to the mind-set that Secretaries General should bring to the office. Hence, it is recommended here that at every stage of the process—in calling for nominations, in establishing the search committee, in interviewing candidates, and in selecting a nominee—the virtues of resolving the tensions between the centralizing dynamics represented by the UN and the decentralizing dynamics represented by the sovereignty principle in favor of the former be articulated and highlighted.

This is not to ignore the very real constraints within which Secretaries General and other UN executives must perform their tasks. There is no question, for example, that the present constitution of the UN system restricts the maneuverability of Secretaries General through the requirement that they be elected and reelected by the UN member states. And even if they are unconcerned about reelection, or if the system is adjusted to protect maneuverability by lengthening the term and forbidding reelection, Secretaries General will nonetheless need the support of the member states if their programmatic initiatives are to bear fruit. Furthermore, even if a Secretary General's policies should prevail in one situation, there is always the danger that in future situations he or she will not receive the support of key member states whose interests had been thwarted in the previous situation.

In short, the executive heads of UN agencies are not comparable to the political leaders of governments. The UN Charter does not accord them the leverage that chiefs of state or prime ministers enjoy under national constitutions. Accordingly, as the case of Amadou-Mahtar M'Bow, a recent Director General of UNESCO, so plainly reveals,[68] UN executives must perforce press new policy initiatives and the idea of expanded UN roles gingerly, exercising care not to win a battle while losing the war. Put differently, the confrontations between Secretaries General and strong governments cannot be so dramatic as to diminish confidence in their leadership.

But constraints are not the same as prohibitions. The UN Charter does not say the Secretary General cannot be innovative in forming support blocs, in playing interests off against each other, in mobilizing actors in the multi-centric world on behalf of policy initiatives, in using available bargaining chips to advance new programs, in earning the confidence of states through frequent and close association with their leaders, or in locating himself or herself on the boards of key NGO groups of scientists, parliamentarians, and other relevant interest groups. All these activities are feasible. The Charter may not have contemplated any leeway in these regards, but the daily routines of UN politics do allow room for a variety of informal moves that the Secretary General can choose to pursue or not. Those moves have to be implemented with circumspection and with a keen appreciation of what can realistically be accomplished, but the choice to interpret executive prerogatives in this way is available.

RECOMMENDATION 6:
ENLARGING THE BULLY PULPIT

But the Secretary General cannot, obviously, do everything that has to be done. Even if he or she is a gifted administrator, and even if the recommended expansion of the Secretariat's top-level staff were to occur, the burdens of the job would continue to be enormous, perhaps exceeding what any single official can effectively shoulder. Furthermore, there are certain tasks that only the official at the top of the UN structure can perform. Most notably, while other administrators can take responsibility for the expanded involvement in domestic elections, nascent conflicts, and the proposed new network of UN missions in foreign capitals, only the Secretary General is endowed with the moral authority needed to bring about the attitude changes called for in Recommendation 1. Clearly, however, it will require more than occasional and sporadic efforts to generate new orientations toward the UN high in national governments. Envisioned here is a task that necessitates endless articulation, sustained attention, considerable travel, and prolonged discussions. Attitudes do not change easily. The old orientations must be continually challenged and expressions of the new ones must be continually reinforced.

Although there can be no substitute for the Secretary General's authority in nursing the new attitudes into place, his or her efforts in this regard can be supplemented. The bully pulpit can be expanded, and the way to do this is by creating, say, five new Deputy Secretaries General (or UN Ambassadors-at-Large) whose sole task would be that of visiting national capitals and engaging chiefs of state, foreign secretaries, media executives, and other key elites in dialogues about the need to replace the outworn give-states-the-benefit-of-the-doubt approach with a vigorous times-require-that-states-go-along philosophy. Those appointed to these new positions would be drawn from the ranks of well-known and widely respected former chiefs of state and foreign secretaries who would find it compelling to tap off their careers on behalf of the UN. The activities of former US President Jimmy Carter since leaving the White House are illustrative of the decent energy that holding high office can generate. Or consider the impact of Eleanor Roosevelt during her years at the UN: a worldwide figure, she focused attention on the organization in ways that few others could or, one might add, have in subsequent years. The impact of former US Secretary of State Cyrus Vance as a special envoy charged with facilitating an end to Yugoslavia's civil war is another good example of how the talents of former national leaders can be enlisted to advance the UN's goals. Of course, the new Deputy Secretaries General would probability not want to hold the office for very long, but a high turnover rate should not present a serious problem inasmuch as it ought to be possible to build up a large pool of distinguished former officials drawn from every region of the world.

If possible, the appointments of these officials should result from a process where they are recommended by the Secretary General and approved by the General Assembly. The latter step would give the appointments legitimacy beyond that which would accrue if only the Secretary General made them. Furthermore, by involving the General Assembly in the process, the idea of developing a new conception of the UN would gain added momentum in the state-centric world. It is possible, of course, that this momentum would be viewed by some states as threatening and therefore result in a sufficient number of negative votes to undermine particular appointments. Grievances accumulated while the candidates for the UN posts held positions high in their national governments might also serve to swell the total of nays. Whatever the outcome of the votes, however, the very controversy over such appointments would serve to focus attention on the bully pulpit and its central message. And if worst came to worst, a back-up procedure that would allow the Secretary General to make the appointment independently could be used.

The more the new appointees could use the bully pulpit by casting the desired new perspectives in concrete terms, the more effective they would likely be. Clearly, not much would be accomplished if they spent their time just calling on heads of governments and urging them in abstract terms to raise their sights and adopt a times-require-that-states-go-along philosophy. Whatever may be the prevailing issues on the global agenda at any time, however, these could readily be interpreted in the context of this philosophy as well as in conventional national-interest terms. Indeed, it may well be that the new Deputy Secretaries General could give voice to interpretations of specific situations that others dare not express, a function that is precisely one of the goals that a bully pulpit is well designed to serve.

Consider, for example, the dilemma in which Germany and Japan found themselves during the Gulf War. Both governments were legally prohibited from an extensive military involvement in the conflict and both were faced with considerable domestic opposition to constitutional revision that would permit direct involvement. A compelling solution to this problem, one that would in the future serve both countries, the UN, and other interested parties, can be found in Article 43 of the UN Charter. It allows for member states to negotiate agreements with the organization whereby national forces are made available, on call, to the Security Council for cases like the Gulf crisis. No country has ever negotiated such an agreement, so that Germany and Japan could be the first to do so. Since they would then be fulfilling a solemn treaty obligation under the UN Charter, domestic opponents in both countries would be hard pressed to successfully contest the agreement and at the same time the two countries would be able to move more securely onto the world stage. But how to launch the idea and give it the kind of impetus that can take off and culminate in a major international development? As it stands, the idea surfaced in an op-ed piece by a distinguished student of the UN,[69] but it never got otherwise championed by politicians and journalists, with the result that it has yet to move onto the global agenda. Conceivably, the proposed new UN officials could provide the needed stimulus. They would have the status, the knowledge, and the perseverance needed to propel such items onto the global agenda. And even if they did not agree among themselves about the merits of the idea, their differences might have the same consequence, perhaps even stimulating enough controversy to generate worldwide pressure on Germany and Japan to negotiate an agreement with the UN.

In short, at a time of rapid change, when new ideas and practices have become acceptable and even commonplace, the potential of the bully pulpit—of voices that give meaning to longings for revised structures and new orientations—can easily be underestimated. And if it is institutionalized in such a way that distinguished world leaders are ready to mount its steps and exhort their former colleagues in national governments to elevate their sights, there is no guessing what it might accomplish.

6

CAUTION, CONFIDENCE, AND FUNDING

I return, in conclusion, to the concern that the recommended policies intended to capitalize on the UN's potential as a change agent derive more from raw idealism than a realistic assessment of the underpinnings of world politics. Is it undue optimism, sheer naiveté, to posit a trendline that ascribes greater authority, competence, effectiveness, and status to the UN? The question is haunting for those whose analytic antennae tell them that fundamental change is at work even as their deepest convictions tell them that this trendline ought to exist. The fear that convictions are driving analysis, however, is no reason to back away from the latter. One introduces caution, stresses that huge problems remain and can well divert the trendline in negative directions, reconsiders the evidence of where turbulent conditions are leading world politics, digs still deeper for signs that observations are not values in disguise, pauses one final time to make sure one's analytic skills are in full command, and then concludes yet again that such a trendline may in fact be operative, that the UN has proven itself highly adaptive across nearly half a century, and that the onset of global turbulence has enlarged and not engulfed the UN.

Renewed confidence in the central thrust of the analysis, however, does not warrant avoidance of the huge problems that persist. Not only is the sovereignty principle alive and well, still propelling officials and publics to define their interests in narrow terms, still tempting them to withhold support for international norms and organizations, but there is also the inescapable reality that the world is broke, that the funds needed to address the many global challenges that threaten to overwhelm individuals, communities, and nations simply do not exist. Indeed, one obstacle to the recommended proliferation of UN missions and tasks is how

77

they will be financed. To call on every member of the UN to donate the resources needed to sustain a mission in its capital, and to argue for a large expansion in the personnel of the organization, is to pile new requirements onto national budgets that are already under siege. And the UN's budget, too, has long been troubled by deficits derived from a combination of expanding commitments and members unwilling to pay their share.[70]

How, then, to generate the resources needed to implement the foregoing recommendations? In part, the question can be easily answered. Four of the recommendations (1, 3, 5, and 6) do not require funds so much as they do shifted priorities and changed attitudes. These activities, of course, are not free of cost in the sense that there will be a need to pay for the time of those who undertake to inculcate the new perspectives; but relatively speaking these costs are minimal and are likely to diminish once the momentum toward reorientation gets under way. Recommendations 2 and 4, on the other hand, cannot be so readily bypassed. They entail charges that will be substantial for many countries and, if successfully implemented, they will continue as annual fees. Hopefully the task of paying for the recommended assumption of new tasks, missions, and personnel by the UN will be at least partially solved by a growing appreciation, reinforced through systematic educational campaigns, that the costs of the UN not expanding in these ways will be greater for each country than those associated with the expansion. It can be readily demonstrated, for example, that expanded peacekeeping operations by the UN that relieve tension-racked countries of maintaining security at their borders, or coping with the fallout of rigged, violent-prone elections, are far less expensive than relentless and endless strife.

Another partial solution to the funding problem can be developed through shifting some of the financial burden to actors in the multi-centric world. They, after all, would benefit indirectly from the attitude changes and greater authority that enable the UN to be more effective, and they would benefit directly from the establishment of UN missions in their state capitals and the recruitment of personnel to operate the missions. So there are good reasons to call for voluntary contributions from the sovereignty-free actors who interface with the UN or, if such a precedent fails to become entrenched, to charge them fees for the services provided by the missions.

Assuming that the financial challenges can be met, there remains the underlying problem that, as the parametric changes continue to unwind and as the UN looms ever larger, more than a few leaders and publics around the world will cling to the assertion that the organization has deviated sharply from its original purposes and functions. Change and transformation, some will surely contend, ought not be allowed to deflect the UN from its historic role as simply a forum in which the state-centric world can contain or resolve its conflicts. But let those who regret and resist the processes of maturation whereby the UN becomes ever more fully woven into the fabric of world politics be reminded of the primordial human condition wherein compliant children grow to be their own persons, often defying their lineage even as they retain some of the original qualities with which they entered the world. And let them reflect, too, on the goals and aspirations that gave birth to the UN; if they do, they will surely conclude that the founders envisioned an organization that would be both adaptive and creative, both in tune with changing times and able to steer the changes to the benefit of peoples everywhere.

NOTES

This paper was prepared with the encouragement and support of the International Peace Academy. A number of people have provided valuable feedback after reading earlier drafts. Hence I am pleased to express my appreciation, though it should be understood that I am solely responsible for the present draft and that none of its faults should be attributed to any of the following: Chadwick F. Alger, Alan Castle, Robert W. Cox, Mary H. Durfee, Giulio M. Gallarotti, Elizabeth Hanson, Daniel Holly, Lawrence S. Finkelstein, Margaret P. Karns, Gunnar Nielsson, Augustus Richard Norton, Pauline Rosenau, John Gerard Ruggie, and two anonymous reviewers for the International Peace Academy.

1. Quoted in Clyde Haberman, "U.N. Takes Over from U.S. at the Kurdish Camp in Iraq," *New York Times*, May 14, 1991, p. A10.

2. Paul Lewis, "UN Votes to Condemn Handling of Iraq Rebels," *New York Times*, April 6, 1991, p. 6.

3. There are, of course, noteworthy exceptions to the tendency to focus undue attention on the internal workings of IOs at the cost of neglecting the stimuli to which they are exposed by a changing world. See, for example, David Mitrany, *A Working Peace System* (Chicago: Quadrangle Books, 1966).

4. Stanley Foundation, *Report of a Vantage Conference: The United Nations' Impact on International Relations* (Muscatine, Iowa: The Stanley Foundation, 1985).

5. J. Martin Rochester, "The Rise and Fall of International Organization as a Field of Study," *International Organization*, Vol. 40 (Autumn 1986), p. 797.

6. Ernst B. Haas, *Why We Still Need the United Nations: The Collective Management of International Conflict, 1945–1984* (Berkeley: Institute of International Studies, University of California, Policy Papers in International Affairs No. 26, 1986), p. 1.

7. Thomas G. Weiss, "Editor's Note," in T.G. Weiss (ed.), *The United Nations in Conflict Management: American, Soviet and Third World Views* (New York: International Peace Academy, 1990), p. 9.

8. An extensive enumeration of the anomalies that surfaced in the 1980s can be found in James N. Rosenau, *Turbulence in World Politics: A*

Theory of Change and Continuity (Princeton: Princeton University Press, 1990), passim.

9. John Lukacs, "The Short Century—It's Over," *New York Times*, February 17, 1991, Sec. 4, p. 13.

10. For the historical analysis that underlies this conclusion, see Rosenau, *Turbulence in World Politics*, Chap. 5.

11. Cf. Vivien A. Schmidt, *Democratizing France: The Political and Administrative History of Decentralization* (Cambridge: Cambridge University Press, 1991).

12. For an extensive discussion of how the sovereignty principle got redefined—how "decolonization amounted to nothing less than an international revolution . . . in which traditional assumptions about the right to sovereign statehood were turned upside down"—in the processes of decolonialization, see Robert H. Jackson, *Quasi-states: Sovereignty, International Relations and the Third World* (Cambridge: Cambridge University Press, 1990), Chap. 4 (the quotation is from p. 85).

13. For an explanation of why the terms "sovereignty-free" and sovereignty-bound" seem appropriate to differentiate between state and nonstate actors, see Rosenau, *Turbulence in World Politics*, p. 36.

14. For a cogent analysis of some of the difficulties encountered by the UN as a consequence of the proliferation of actors in both the state- and multi-centric worlds, see Harold K. Jacobson, William M. Reisinger, and Todd Mathers, "National Entanglements in International Governmental Organizations," *American Political Science Review*, Vol. 80 (March 1986), pp. 141–59.

15. Nor is the pace of technological advance slowing down. It is estimated that by the end of the century new generations of supercomputers will be capable of calculating more than a trillion operations each second. Cf. "Transforming the Decade: 10 Critical Technologies," *New York Times*, December 1, 1991, p. 18.

16. The first night of the Gulf War CNN's prime-time viewership went from its normal 560,000 to 11,400,000. Cf. Thomas B. Rosenstiel, "CNN: The Channel to the World," *Los Angeles Times*, January 23, 1991, p. A12.

17. An account of *Actuel*'s efforts can be found in *Europe: Magazine of the European Community* (April 1990), pp. 40–41.

18. For an extensive elaboration of the diverse ways in which the microelectronic revolution has impacted on the conduct of public affairs, see Rosenau, *Turbulence in World Politics*, Chap. 13.

19. For an insightful account of how the UN can engage in productive interactions with actors in the multi-centric world, see Kathryn Sikkink, "Codes of Conduct for Transnational Corporations: The Case of the WHO/UNICEF Code," *International Organization*, Vol. 40 (Autumn 1986), pp. 815–40.

20. See, for example, Ted Robert Gurr, "War, Revolution and the Growth of the Coercive State," in James A. Caporaso (ed.), *The Elusive State: International and Comparative Perspectives* (Newbury Park, Calif.: Sage Publications, 1989), pp. 49–68.

21. For discussions along these lines, see James N. Rosenau, "The State in an Era of Cascading Politics: Wavering Concept, Widening Competence, Withering Colossus, or Weathering Change?" in Caporaso, *The Elusive State*, pp. 17–48, and Giulio M. Gallarotti, "Legitimacy as a Capital Asset of the State," *Public Choice*, Vol. 63 (1989), pp. 43–61.

22. Tara Sonenshine, "The Revolution Has Been Televised," *Washington Post National Weekly Edition,* October 8–14, 1990, p. 29.

23. An account of the loyalty and membership problems faced by Norway can be found in William E. Schmidt, "Norway Again Debates European Membership, Rekindling Old Hostilities," *New York Times,* May 6, 1991, p. A3.

24. The quotes are taken from Alan Riding, "France Questions Its Identity as It Sinks into 'Le Malaise,'" *New York Times,* December 23, 1990, pp. 1, 7.

25. In some instances the movement can be both upward and downward. Present-day Croatia, with its aspiration both to secede from Yugoslavia and to join the European Community, is a case in point.

26. The conception of Third World countries as quasi-states can be found in Jackson, *Quasi-states,* Chaps. 1 and 7.

27. For a useful delineation between positive and negative sovereignty, see Jackson, *Quasi-states,* pp. 26–31.

28. I am indebted to Daniel Holly for calling my attention, in personal correspondence, to the Third World perspective that the "entire United Nations system works mainly to the benefit of those states and groups at the center of the world system" and that therefore "the proposals contained in the last part of the paper are very idealistic . . . [in assuming] a world exempt from domination, a world in which the interests of every group will be taken care of."

29. Bruce Russett and James S. Sutterlin, "The U.N. in a New World Order," *Foreign Affairs,* Vol. 70 (Spring 1991), p. 70. The elasticity mentioned in this quote refers to the UN's peacekeeping activities, but extending the observation to all of its activities does not seem inappropriate.

30. Perhaps because they are only marginal interdependence issues, those involving trade stand out as an exception in this regard. Trade relations, it seems clear, are moving steadily in the direction of bloc rather than global arrangements.

31. Chiang Pei-heng, *Nongovernmental Organizations at the United Nations* (New York: Praeger Publishers, 1981), p. 7.

32. The UN organ responsible for liaison with NGOs is the Economic and Social Council (ECOSOC), which has procedures and eligibility requirements for accrediting NGOs that accord them scaled rights of access to and participation in UN deliberations. I have been unable to locate authoritative statistics on the number of NGOs approved by all UN agencies, but some notion of their scope can be seen in the fact that ECOSOC accredited 2,696 NGOs in 1976. For one attempt to scale the importance of NGOs by the extent of their recognition by IOs, see Harold K. Jacobson, *Networks of Interdependence* (New York: Alfred A. Knopf, 1979), pp. 435–39. Other assessments of their influence can be found in Chiang Pei-heng, *Nongovernmental Organizations at the United Nations,* and Peter Willetts (ed.), *Pressure Groups in the Global System: The Transnational Relations of Issue-Oriented Nongovernmental Organizations* (London: Frances Pinter, 1982).

33. I am indebted to Lawrence S. Finkelstein for pointing out in personal correspondence that movement into the vacuum can occur in either of two ways: the Secretary General can respond to situations without the consent of the involved states or, alternatively, without the permission of a UN organ. Although a politically acceptable tradition has accumulated, started by Dag Hammarskjöld and asserted by all his successors, wherein the

Secretary General may respond to a situation without the authorization of a UN organ if invited to do so by a state, the vacuum nonetheless remains in the case of situations where neither a state nor the Security Council or General Assembly sanctions the Secretary General's involvement.

34. Ernst B. Haas, *When Knowledge Is Power: Three Models of Change in International Organizations* (Berkeley: University of California Press, 1990), p. 181.

35. Johan Galtung, "On the Anthropology of the United Nations System," in David Pitt and Thomas G. Weiss (eds.), *The Nature of United Nations Bureaucracies* (Boulder: Westview Press, 1986), pp. 2, 14.

36. Lawrence S. Finkelstein, "The Politics of Value Allocation in the UN System," in L.S. Finkelstein (ed.), *Politics in the United Nations System* (Durham: Duke University Press, 1988), pp. 5, 30.

37. For one effort to pull together diagrammatically all the units of the UN system and the tenure specifications of their executive heads, see Brian Urquhart and Erskine Childers, *A World in Need of Leadership: Tomorrow's United Nations* (Uppsala, Sweden: Dag Hammarskjöld Foundation, 1990), pp. 90–91.

38. Robert W. Cox, Harold K. Jacobson, et al., *The Anatomy of Influence* (New Haven: Yale University Press, 1976), pp. 420–23.

39. Finkelstein, "The Politics of Value Allocation in the UN System," p. 12.

40. Lawrence S. Finkelstein, "Comparative Politics in the UN System," in Finkelstein, *Politics in the United Nations System*, p. 450.

41. See John Mueller, *Retreat from Doomsday: The Obsolescence of Major War* (New York: Basic Books, 1989).

42. For an analysis of the juxtaposition of these six developments, see James N. Rosenau, "Interdependence and the Simultaneity Puzzle: Notes on the Outbreak of Peace," in Charles W. Kegley, Jr. (ed.), *The Long Postwar Peace: Contending Explanations and Projections* (New York: HarperCollins Publishers, 1991), pp. 307–328.

43. I undertake a full discussion of the diminishing probabilities of interstate war in "A Wherewithal for Revulsion: Notes on the Obsolescence of Interstate War," a paper presented at the annual meeting of the American Political Science Association, Washington, D.C., August 30, 1991. For a creative effort to measure the UN's success with respect to war-peace issues, see Haas, *Why We Still Need the United Nations*, esp. Chap. 2.

44. A cogent discussion of the fragile nature of sovereignty in the Third World can be found in Jackson, *Quasi-states*, Chap. 2.

45. See, for example, Brian Urquhart, "Sovereignty vs. Suffering," *New York Times*, April 17, 1991, p. A15; Jonathan Mann, "No Sovereignty for Suffering," *New York Times*, April 12, 1991, Sec. 4, p. 17; and editorial, "The U.N. Must Deal with Kurds' Plight," *Los Angeles Times*, April 30, 1991, p. B6.

46. For an account of one situation in which the UN did act on the basis of humanitarian imperatives rather than acceding to the sovereignty principle, see Thomas G. Weiss and Larry Minear, "Do International Ethics Matter?: Humanitarian Politics in the Sudan," *Ethics and International Affairs*, Vol. 5 (1991), pp. 197–214.

47. Mann, "No Sovereignty for Suffering."

48. Haas, *Why We Still Need the United Nations*, p. 68.

49. Sidney Dell, *The United Nations and International Business* (Durham: Duke University Press, 1991), p. ix.

50. I am indebted to Giulio M. Gallarotti for pointing out, in a personal communication, at least one offsetting factor that may lead people to be increasingly critical of the UN. This involves a tendency of governmental leaders to avoid the costs of onerous tasks by shifting them to IOs, with the result that the performances of the latter are evaluated with respect to tasks that allow little room for unqualified success. The selection-of-task bias may load against the probability of outstanding performances. For an extended analysis of this point, see Roland Vaubel, "A Public Choice Approach to International Organization," *Public Choice*, Vol. 51 (1986), pp. 39–57.

51. I am indebted to Chadwick F. Alger for these data.

52. Dell, The United Nations and International Business, p. ix.

53. For an extended analysis of the processes of aggregation that culminate in collectivities that are more than the sum of their parts, see Rosenau, *Turbulence in World Politics*, Chap. 7. For an analysis that, in effect argues that the UN does not add to a sum greater than its parts, that it lacks a unity of purpose and thus "is just one other context in which competing national interests are pursued," see Alan James, "The Security Council: Paying for Peacekeeping," in David P. Forsythe (ed.), *The United Nations in the World Political Economy: Essays in Honour of Leon Gordenker* (New York: St. Martin's Press, 1989), p. 14.

54. Augustus Richard Norton and Thomas George Weiss, *UN Peace-keepers: Soldiers with a Difference* (New York: Foreign Policy Association, 1990), p. 50.

55. Richard Marin, "The Winners in the War: Bush, Republicans and the U.N.," *Washington Post National Weekly Edition*, March 18–24, 1991, p. 38.

56. Tom Wicker, "What Kind of Order?" *New York Times*, June 8, 1991, p. 23.

57. This account and the quotes are drawn from Clyde Haberman, "U.N. Enters a City to Assure Kurds," *New York Times*, May 20, 1991, p. A6.

58. For a cogent account of the UN as a change agent in the environmental field, see Donald J. Puchala, "The United Nations and Ecosystem Issues: Institutionalizing the Global Interest," in Finkelstein, *Politics in the United Nations System*, pp. 214–45. An extensive but more general inquiry into IOs as both adaptive entities and agents of change can be found in Haas, *When Knowledge Is Power*.

59. Puchala, "The United Nations and Ecosystem Issues," pp. 225–26.

60. Arthur R. Day, "Conclusion: A Mix of Means," in A.R. Day and M.W. Doyle (eds.), *Escalation and Intervention: Multilateral Security and Its Alternatives* (Boulder: Westview Press, 1986), pp. 156–61.

61. In *Turbulence in World Politics* (pp. 32–33) I conceptualize change on this order in terms of JND's—Just Noticeable Differences—that are significant even if they are not necessarily substantial. Given the extraordinary complexity of world politics, changes that involve only one JND can hardly be discounted.

62. See Giulio M. Gallarotti, "The Limits of International Organization: Systematic Failure in the Management of International Relations," *International Organization*, Vol. 45 (Spring 1991), pp. 192–93.

63. It should be noted that the reputation for evenhandedness cannot be located exclusively in the hands of the UN's missions abroad. Even if the field personnel greatly enhanced the reputation for fairness, much would also depend on the political processes of the General Assembly, the Security Council, and the legislative organs of other agencies. If these membership

bodies were consistently to exhibit an unyielding bias toward certain countries, then no amount of good will generated in the field would be sufficient to counterbalance a negative reputation.

64. Rosenau, *Turbulence in World Politics*, Chap. 16.

65. This is not the first time this suggestion has been made. For more extensive formulations of it, see Johan Galtung, *The True Worlds: A Transnational Perspective* (New York: Free Press, 1980), pp. 346–50, and Richard Falk, "A Postmodern Presidency for a Postmodern World," paper presented at the Conference for a Postmodern World, Santa Barbara, 1989.

66. Cf. David Pitt, "Power in the UN Superbureacracy: A Modern Byzantium?" in Pitt and Weiss, *The Nature of United Nations Bureaucracies*, pp. 23–38.

67. See, for example, Urquhart and Childers, *A World in Need of Leadership*, and Report of the 22nd United Nations Issues Conference, *The United Nations: Structure and Leadership for a New Era* (Muscatine, Iowa: The Stanley Foundation, 1991), pp. 13–16.

68. Lawrence S. Finkelstein, "The Political Role of the Director-General of UNESCO," in Finkelstein, *Politics in the United Nations System*, pp. 385–423.

69. John Gerard Ruggie, "Use U.N. to Ease into a Global Role," *The Japan Times*, April 10, 1991.

70. For a discussion of the problems and processes involved in funding UN projects, see Alan James, "The Security Council: Paying for Peacekeeping," in Forsythe, *The United Nations in the World Political Economy*, pp. 13–35, and Susan R. Mills, *The Financing of United Nations Peacekeeping Operations: The Need for a Sound Financial Basis* (New York: International Peace Academy, 1989).

ABOUT THIS OCCASIONAL PAPER

While studies of the United Nations typically focus on its internal procedures, resources, and problems, this path-breaking inquiry probes the UN's external circumstances—the diverse ways in which the rapidly changing international scene is likely to both provide it with opportunities and impose constraints.

Rosenau's bifurcation model of global turbulence suggests the emergence of a series of power gaps that may well be filled by the United Nations in the years ahead. His analysis highlights the probability that, far from being engulfed by change, the world organization seems destined to be enlarged by it. He offers, as well, six specific recommendations for policies through which the UN can become not only a recipient, but also an agent, of change.

JAMES N. ROSENAU is director of the Institute of Transnational Studies at the University of Southern California. A former president of the International Studies Association, Professor Rosenau was awarded a Guggenheim Fellowship in 1987 and subsequently wrote *Turbulence in World Politics: A Theory of Change and Continuity*, which in turn gave rise to the present monograph on how the conditions of turbulence have affected the UN. His first play, *Kwangju: An Escalatory Spree*, was produced in the fall of 1991 in Los Angeles.

THE INTERNATIONAL PEACE ACADEMY

The International Peace Academy is an independent, nonpartisan, international institution devoted to the promotion of peaceful and multilateral approaches and to the resolution of international as well as internal conflicts. IPA plays a facilitating role in efforts to settle conflicts, providing a middle ground where the options for resolving particular conflicts are explored in an informal, off-the-record setting. Other activities of the organization focus on public forums; training seminars on conflict resolution and peacekeeping; and research and workshops on collective security, regional and internal conflicts, peacemaking, peacekeeping, and nonmilitary aspects of security.

In fulfilling its mission, IPA works closely with the United Nations, regional and other international organizations, governments, and parties to conflicts. The work of IPA is enhanced by its ability to draw on a worldwide network of eminent persons comprising statesmen, business leaders, diplomats, military officers, and scholars. In the aftermath of the Cold War, there is a general awakening to the enormous potential of peaceful and multilateral approaches to resolving conflicts. This has given renewed impetus to the role of IPA.

IPA is governed by an international board of directors. Financial support for the work of the organization is provided primarily by philanthropic foundations, as well as individual donors.

INTERNATIONAL PEACE ACADEMY

OCCASIONAL PAPER SERIES

Available from the International Peace Academy, 777 United Nations Plaza, New York, New York 10017 (212-949-8480):

> *The Future of Peacekeeping*, Indar Jit Rikhye
> *Paths to Peace in Afghanistan: The Geneva Accords and After*, Selig S. Harrison
> *The Financing of United Nations Peacekeeping Operations: The Need for a Sound Financial Basis*, Susan R. Mills
> *United Nations Peacekeeping: Management and Operations*, F. T. Liu
> *Negotiations Before Peacekeeping*, Cameron R. Hume

Available from Lynne Rienner Publishers, 1800 30th Street, Boulder, Colorado 80301 (303-444-6684):

> *The United Nations in a Turbulent World*, James N. Rosenau
> *United Nations Peacekeeping and the Nonuse of Force*, F. T. Liu

"James Rosenau's welcome speculation about the emerging prospects for the United Nations, based on his stimulating hypotheses about turbulence in the international system, is intelligently provocative and always interesting. . . . The policy-oriented suggestions as to some ways the UN might serve as an 'agent of change,' with which Rosenau ends the work, are especially provocative."

—Lawrence S. Finkelstein

"Professor Rosenau provides a succinct portrait of a dramatically changing world and then thoughtfully illuminates how this 'turbulent world' presents opportunities for creative thinking on how the UN can be a major change agent."—Chadwick F. Alger

ISBN: 1-55587-330-8